PRAISE FOR ANNE WHITEHOUSE'S POETRY

OUTSIDE FROM THE INSIDE

"*Outside from the Inside* is a book about joy, grief, and transcendence. Whitehouse writes in the spirit of Bob Kaufman, the Beat Poet and Buddhist who is quoted in the book's epigraph... Like Kaufman, who wrote in mantra-like rhythms and jazz-infused incantations, Whitehouse often celebrates the pleasures of physical being -- heartbeats, drumbeats, dance steps, trance-like contemplation of the ocean in ourselves, and altered states of consciousness. In steady, end-stopped cadences, against a backdrop of rivers and forests, Whitehouse weaves narratives about workers, farmers, healers, artists, and musicians that reckon with human cruelty and folly, but are leavened by wisdom and discipline.

"In stunning poems about organs, muscles, and bones, Whitehouse brings to bear on the lyric poem the lexicon of human anatomy...'The Essence of Trees,' which considers the passion and practice of the poet's Aunt Louise, who cultivated bonsai, is an *ars poetica*... The poem describes the 'careful work of repotting each tree,' finding and trimming its root. One can spend a lifetime cultivating an art or answering a calling that may seem to the world at large nothing more or less than learning how to trim a bonsai root...These poems benefit from the methodical steadfastness of the poet, who knows what it means to thrive even when given a small container. Trimming the feeding root, starting from the inside, and removing the old, dry foliage are apt metaphors for Whitehouse's practice, as is the discovery that '(n)o pine is like another.' This book reminds us, even in an age of class war, plague, and rampant materialism, that dedication, method, focus, and the pursuit of beauty offer far more satisfaction than anything we can buy or own."   -HILARY SIDERIS, *American Book Review*

"Evoking the small act of kindness, the overlooked muscles of connection, the sounds and words of the past, the poet demonstrates how these things sustain us.... There is a moral imperative at work here, grounded in seeing the other —whether a Vietnamese child, a shopkeeper who has lost his life's dream, a lonely grandmother aching for beauty, or a tired hawk at rest."

-NANCY LUDMERER, *Streetlight Magazine*

"*Outside from the Inside* ranges far in persona and place, from My Lai to the Mackinac Bridge to the Canyon de Chelly to New Orleans; from a survivor who works with troubled youth to Hemingway's second wife, to 'generations of rabbis'…The theme of beauty in nature and art permeates the poems and the cover artwork which appears to be an Asian wall hanging in oranges, greens, and tans and crammed with people, symbols, and plants, a full and rich array just like the poems within.   -DIANE KENDIG, *Charge Magazine*

Outside From the Inside is a many-legged thing…like Whitman's spider launching 'filament, filament, filament, out of itself'…Lines like 'Here, there is a memory / of ancient places, / wind and sun, endlessness, / where I came from, / and where I will go. …' align with both Noguchi's expression of wind, flight and movement as well as the core mood of the book – a poetics wrapped up in being *placed by moments*. Emphasizing this paradoxy – in the sense that moments always seem to pick up and move on – *Outside From the Inside* ends on a nicely juxtaposed note, placing the small alongside the large: "Oh, for an orange, / Oh, for the sea." Whitehouse borrows these lines from the real Noguchi letter. It is in details like this where I think Whitehouse is most successful… *Outside from the Inside* left me feeling…a little more placed, on 'a gray road like a fallen ribbon.'

-EVAN NICHOLLS, *Editions Bibliotekos*

SURREALIST MUSE and *ESCAPING LEE MILLER*

The generosity and thoughtfulness with which Whitehouse represents both of these incredible women and their art shows that not only is she an admirer of their work, but that her own writing could belong to the same era-defying worlds that Miller and Carrington found themselves to be a part of....It is as though Whitehouse has stepped into her own occult to channel both these women and tell their stories.   -LAURA SALVATORE, *Open: Journal of Arts & Letters*

METEOR SHOWER

"*Meteor Shower* is truly a stunning and moving collection of poetry. The shifts from section to section show a beautiful trajectory, down into memory and loss, back into engagement with the present, and finally a movement upward towards transcendence and infinity. The poems grapple, often intensely with loss and dislocation, and yet there is a sense of purpose to the pain. As one line in 'Creativity' captures well about the collection as a whole: 'An accident will lead you to creation.' Yes, indeed, it does."   -IAN MALONEY, *Editions Bibliotekos*

"For several years now, through a series of thoughtful and quietly beautiful books, Anne Whitehouse has proven herself to be among the most astute and substantial poets working in the United States. It is difficult think of another writer who is able to combine delicate, pitch-perfect lyricism with such urgent personal material. Whitehouse's talents and her gentle wisdom are on full display in her latest collection *Meteor Shower*, a book that may be her most personal yet—and her most affecting."   -JOHN VANDERSLICE, *Alabama Writers Forum*

"Anne Whitehouse's "Calligraphies" was a hands-down favorite from the moment I read it… In a seemingly effortless manner, Whitehouse carries the reader along with details of another time and another culture even as her poem encompasses the way history can shape lives and challenge the human psyche."   -CAROL HAMILTON, Judge, 2016 *Songs of Eretz* poetry prize

THE REFRAIN

"Anne Whitehouse's poems locate moments of transformation when the old life mutates irrevocably into a new form, moments of

terror and confusion followed by clarity and the possibility of a new beginning....Reading *The Refrain* is a rewarding and humanizing experience, like the experience of reading a good novel. We enter the lives of others in language that allows us to connect with and appreciate their challenges, broadening and deepening our own humanity."
-MARY KAISER, *Alabama Writers Forum*

"These poems portray exactly what they intend to portray, true feelings and a quest to understand our physical and spiritual existence. Whitehouse's personal narratives and meditations...are never elevated beyond the believable, yet they achieve a unique effect in their persistent attempt to discover and reveal the subtlety of experience. Her subjects are drawn from nature, from stories and observations of people, and from her own meditations... Whitehouse doesn't judge, and she never gives too much, but she always gives us something that sticks.

"Outside all of this conjecture is her great poem 'The Beyond.' Written from the point of view of a woman who has lost her husband in the Twin Towers inferno and collapse, here is a poem that succeeds in every way. The language is subtle and balanced and for two and a half pages sustains its precision and potency without ever being sentimental or excessive. The poem's images are indelible, and its meanings are many-leveled and powerful."
-RON GASKILL, *Jerseyworks*

ONE SUNDAY MORNING

"Within the pages of this spellbinding collection, there's an undeniable perplexity and wonderment when observing realities beyond our power....The central theme woven throughout the book is that nature, with its beauty, banality and grandeur, can also be chaotic, unpredictable, and cruel....Granted, this message may be age-old, but the ingenuity in Whitehouse's delivery defies stereotypes, making it fresh and new.... There does not seem to be one extraneous poem in the collection."
-CHERYL SOMMESE, *The Write Place at the Write Time*

BEAR IN MIND

"Anne Whitehouse's 'The Beyond,'—and we say this with confidence— stands alone, and is perhaps one of the best 9/11 poems that we have read. It is truly an exceptional poem—the control exercised by the poetic voice on such a subject of apocalyptic chaos, yet the tenderness and the emotion—with depth as deep…as T.S. Eliot or W.B. Yeats….Through her poetic voice we understand the human (the poet's) predicament and predilection—the act of searching, for something new, to reclaim what has been left behind for us to find."   -GREGORY TAGUE,
Editions Bibliotekos

BLESSINGS AND CURSES

"The fluidity, the rise and fall, the relationships of blessings and curses runs a current through to the last words of the last poem, where a beautiful work of art will be sent back to the waters. But unlike the work of art returning to the sea, or Moses nearing the Promised Land, never to set foot in it ('Blessings and Curses,' the first poem in the book), Blessings and Curses leaves behind a blessing—a rich collection of poetic observation of the balance of life's pleasures and sorrows, a permanence for the reader."   -CARLA DODD, *Troubadour 21*

"Anne Whitehouse's gentle understanding alternates with her astringent anatomizing of character—the mix produces a deeply humane volume that's a bold change from the weightless irony and knowingness of postmodernism."   -DAVID CASTRONOVO, author of *Blokes:
The Bad Boys of British Literature* and other books

Praise for Anne Whitehouse's novel, FALL LOVE

"Whitehouse's poetic handling of language and of sensuous detail is superb: in her descriptions, especially, of the intimacies of lovemaking, she is at the same time graphic and subtle, provocative and sensitive; in her portrayal of the unspoken emotions - about death and its aftermath, of fear, of pride, and of hurt - she conveys powerfully the cruel effects of all those coincidences of life." -ELAINE HUGHES, *First Draft*

"The main characters in Anne Whitehouse's novel, *Fall Love*, are Althea, Jeanne, Paul, and Bryce: four twentysomethings in New York in 1980. And while we meet other characters over the months that the novel takes place, as I read, I found myself feeling that one persistent theme was so integral that, to me, it almost functioned as a character as well. The idea of what it means to be an artist is a theme impels the action throughout the novel and that is returned to again and again in different ways...The initial questions of identity are still there at the novel's end, and if progress has been made, it is uncertain progress. And I didn't really feel as if the story ended: only the part of it that I had been watching." -JENNIFER FINSTROM, *NEAT*

"A restless undercurrent swirls in these pages, charged with poetry, daring, and eroticism alternating with moments of self-reflection. An exploration of the human spirit through a patchwork of emotions, self-interest joined with tenderness in a world of angels and demons." -JUAN CARLOS SILVA,
Universidad Pedagógica y Tecnológica de Colombia,
reviewing *Amigos y amantes*, *Fall Love*'s Spanish translation

STEADY

poems

Anne Whitehouse

DOS MADRES

2023

DOS MADRES PRESS INC.
P.O. Box 294, Loveland, Ohio 45140
www.dosmadres.com   editor@dosmadres.com

Dos Madres is dedicated to the belief that the small press is essential
to the vitality of contemporary literature as a carrier of the new voice,
as well as the older, sometimes forgotten voices of the past. And in an
ever more virtual world, to the creation of fine books pleasing to the
eye and hand.

Dos Madres is named in honor of Vera Murphy and Libbie Hughes,
the "Dos Madres" whose contributions have made this press possible.

Dos Madres Press, Inc. is an Ohio Not For Profit Corporation and a
501 (c) (3) qualified public charity. Contributions are tax deductible.

Executive Editor: Robert J. Murphy

Illustration & Book Design: Elizabeth H. Murphy
www.illusionstudios.net

Typeset in Adobe Garamond Pro & Cochin
ISBN 978-1-953252-83-8
Library of Congress Control Number: 2023938476

ACKNOWLEDGMENTS AND NOTE

Grateful acknowledgment is made to the following journals and anthologies where these poems first appeared:

Amethyst Magazine, Aquifer: The Florida Review Online; Cumberland River Review; Ethel Zine and Micro Press; Evocations: A Literary and Art Review; Exist Otherwise; Falling Star Magazine; Feminine Collective, First Literary Review East; The Greensilk Journal; Hawaii Pacific Review; In Parentheses; Journal of Expressive Writing; Lit 202; Literary Veganism; October Hill Magazine: OJA&L: Open: Journal of Arts and Letters, One Art: A Journal of Poetry; Pensive; Poetry Pacific; Roi Fainéant; Shark Reef; Tipton Poetry Journal; Verse-Virtual; White Enso; Young Ravens Literary Review; Zingara Poets.

"Lady Bird," won the 2023 poetry contest to "Honor American History," sponsored by The Nathan Perry Chapter of the National Society Daughters of the American Revolution of Lorain County, Ohio.

"Being Ruth Asawa" received the 2022 White Enso poetry award.

NOTE: "123 Home Free" was inspired by the novel *Heidi* by Johanna Spyri and by Aaron Fletcher, who recounts his experiences on his youtube channel.

For my teachers

*A man's life of any worth is a continual allegory, and
very few eyes can see the mystery of his life.*

—John Keats,
Letter to George and Georgiana Keats, 1819

TABLE OF CONTENTS

I—MORNING SWIM

II—SIGNS

III—An Art Story

IV—Blue

I

MORNING SWIM

MORNING SWIM

The island sparkles in the morning,
Grasses nodding, leaves waving,
All alive and moving, yet still rooted.

The day passes in sunlight and shadow.
Billowy clouds blow across the sun.
What seems like silence
Is full of sound.
Rocked by gentle waves,
I float between deep blue sky
And dark blue sea,
Bathed in endless waters
That are cold, healing, and bitter.

SNOWDROPS

In memory of Paul Berné

He loved this uncertain time of year,
when the willow fronds
turn pale with promise. It starts
with the knife edge of a winter wind
that tastes of spring,
the lengthening light.
The rains have come, and the moss
is emerald green.
Clumps of snowdrops
are sprouting in unexpected places.
Finding them is like coming across
an old friend after many years.
As if I were greeting Paul,
or glimpsing his ghost
in the delicate arch of each stem
weighted with its white flower.

POND LIVES

One autumn morning
after we bought our land,
I saw dead plants and detritus
floating on the surface of the pond.
I thought someone had sprayed
the water with herbicide.

But it was a natural process.
Cooling water at the surface
grew denser and heavier,
sinking towards the bottom,
and the warmer water below
rose to the top.

The decomposing matter
floating on the surface
emerged from the bottom,
where organisms live off the waste
of fungi, bacteria, and worms.
The autumn winds and rains
mixed up layers of water
that summer had stratified.

As I paddled the canoe,
glimpses of aquatic life
beckoned below me:
a flash of a fish disappearing
in a ruffle of waving weeds,
a turtle paddling towards a log,
snakes, worms, and crabs scuttling
into the rich murk.

In the first week of winter
we watched thousands of geese
whirling and landing and settling,
then flying up again
in great flocks.

At the turn of the year,
deep cold set in.
Under a shroud of ice,
the pond lay sleeping.

From the depths
of hibernation
came the birth
of spring's desire,
sprouting slowly,
yearning upwards
towards spreading
light and warmth.

Summer's invasion of green
occupied pondscape
and landscape.
I swam over rough weeds,
submerged and free-floating,
yet close enough to scratch my skin.

There was coontail and bladderwort,
pondweed and milfoil.
Growing along the surface
were waterlilies and duckweed.

I reached deep water and swam free.
On a dock in the middle of the pond,
two teenagers invited me to join them.
I climbed up the ladder
and sat down beside them.
They were brother and sister.

The dock felt rough
against my wet bathing suit,
as I lay warming in the sun
after the cool water.
I closed my eyes
and let my mind drift.

YAHRZEIT

My parents were rarely on the same wavelength.
Most of the time they talked at each other,
not to each other. But here they are,
by a quirk of the Hebrew calendar,
yoked forever and forever,
until the end of time,
sharing the same *Yahrzeit*,
although one died in February
and the other in March,
two years apart.

Every year I pray for them together
and speak their names together,
before my congregation.

SMUGGLED IMAGES

I

Sister Three was on the phone,
and she was outraged. Sister Two
had told her about the photos
I had taken that afternoon
of our mother lying dead
in the open casket
in the viewing room
of the funeral home.

Sister Three scolded me
for my lack of respect
and demanded I delete the pictures.
She said Sisters One and Two
agreed with her.

We each have our own ways
of grieving, I wanted to say,
but I was too spent to argue.
"All right," I said, "I'll do it."
One by one, I deleted the pictures,
while my daughter, sitting next to me
on the bed in the hotel room,
confirmed it to my sister.
"Okay," she replied, mollified.
I could see she'd been prepared
for an argument I hadn't given her.

As soon as she hung up,
I reinstalled the photos.
"It's none of her business,"
I told my daughter.
"These photos are precious to me."

II

Nearly ten years after my mother's death,
I stare at these last images of her.
She died soon after her cancer diagnosis.
She had no time to waste away.

In my pictures she is lying tranquilly
against the white silk lining
of the casket. Her eyes are closed,
her face is made up, and her hair arranged.
She looks like herself, and yet not
like herself. She is wearing a dress
of navy-blue velvet, and her hands are folded.
On her left wrist is a silver link
bracelet made by Sister One.

I recall the mortician wringing his hands,
speaking softly with the right note of sadness,
yet clearly proud of his handiwork
and eager for us to see what he had done.

An impulse made me take the photos
after he left the room. Even though I knew
I never could solve the mystery of my mother,
I knew I would want to keep these images
close to my heart.

AT TWENTY

At twenty my daughter
expects so much of life
that she is often disappointed.

She hasn't yet learned to ask for less
and be happier with what she has.

I wonder if, in later years,
she will look back
with longing at this time.

IN TANDEM

When we moved into our apartment,
we painted over the ugly wallpaper
in the master bathroom, first with primer,
then with white, oil-based paint
in an eggshell finish.

Using artists' oil pigments
we mixed a Caribbean aquamarine
and thinned it with oil glaze.
With a ribbed cotton cloth,
we ragged the luminous glaze
in gentle swirls over the white walls,
suggesting the depths of the ocean.

My husband created a stencil in mylar
of Hokusai's famous tidal wave
rearing its head like a stallion,
tossing white flecks of spray
like the locks of a horse's mane.

Master of Exakto knives
and mathematic intervals,
my husband sized the stencil
so its repeating pattern
fit the wall's dimensions,
and he cut it flawlessly.

He invented, and I implemented,
balancing on the bathroom counter
to apply the stencil to the walls.

The waves, in dazzling white
and black and dark cobalt,
contrasted with the aquamarine.

To add to the illusion,
we made miniature models
of Caribbean fish in paper maché—
black drum and red snapper,
triggerfish and porgy,
grunt and angelfish,
seahorse with a curved tail—
which we painted realistically
and strung using dental floss
from hooks in the ceiling,
suspended below Hokusai's waves
in the bathroom's watery element.

We didn't know then
about Hokusai and his daughter,
how he recognized her talents
in childhood and fostered them.
She worked alongside him in the studio.
It is said that some of the works
attributed to him were made by her.

In a time and place where women
were confined to the domestic sphere,
did Katsushita Oi's obscurity
trouble her? Her modesty and her sex
were impediments to her renown,
so perhaps she was content to add to his.

POISONS AND MEDICINES

"All things are poisons, and nothing is without poison;
only the dose makes a thing not a poison."
—Paracelsus

During rituals of divination,
Mayan sorcerers and healers
induced risky hallucinations
with *Brugmansia candida*,
angel's trumpet. The poison
in its white, waxy flowers
and dark green leaves,
ingested or absorbed through
the body's mucous membranes,
causes convulsions, paralysis,
coma, and death.

To dilate the pupils of their eyes
and bring a flush to their cheeks,
fashionable ladies in medieval Europe
drank juice pressed from the berries
and leaves of *Atropa belladonna*,
the deadly nightshade.
To enhance their beauty,
they risked their lives with a poison
used since antiquity to alter potions
and tip arrows with lethal results.

Our ancestors felt more closely
than we the embrace
of science and mystery.
We are still looking

for the boundary.
Chemicals crossing
the blood-brain barrier
create effects in the brain
that achieve results in the body,
altering perceptions
of pleasure and pain.
Reliever of illness
or harbinger of death
is a matter of degree.

Digitalis from foxglove,
lily of the valley, and oleander
strengthens the heart's contractions
while causing blurred and double vision
and hallucinations.
Taxol from the bark of the Pacific yew
destroys cancers of the breast
and ovaries but harms the liver.
Although it induces nausea,
vincristine, an alkaloid
from Madagascar periwinkle,
is the reason why most children
with leukemia now survive.

For the stomach spasms
I suffered as a child,
I was prescribed a daily dose
of a chalky green medicine
containing belladonna alkaloids
and phenobarbital
to prevent nausea and relax me.

Derived from salicin
in willow bark and meadowsweet,
aspirin reduces inflammation,
eases headache, and lowers fever.
Years ago, my great-aunt, sick of life,
swallowed the entire contents
of a bottle and bled to death.

MARIE KONDO

Bringing order
into home and workplace
makes room for hope.
Our clutter of things
is a clutter of emotions
that overwhelm us.

Marie Kondo arrives like a fairy
from another realm.
Her black hair, cut neatly
below her ears, shines like silk.
Under her straight bang,
her dark eyes sparkle.
Her smile is infectious.

She is as tiny and pale as a pixie,
yet she is married, with three children.
She wears a pure white blouse,
a full skirt, tights, and ballet slippers.
She laughs her tinkling laugh
and claps her hands together
at the sight of chaos.

She orders clients to bring all they have
out into the open and look at it,
touch it, and own it.
The tangle of clothes in the drawers,
in the closets, on the floor,
the piles of shoes, sports equipment.

The stacks of paper, jumbled books,
magazines, business records,
playbills, and correspondence.

The toys, the tools, the games,
the souvenirs, the family photos,
all the stuff they thought they might use,
and maybe did for a while, or didn't.
Their collections of every kind,
and all the household objects
that seem to accumulate on their own.
Then there are the bathroom
and the kitchen, worlds of their own.

Faced with all the evidence
of their lives, Marie's clients
frequently burst into tears.

Some of them have not looked
at their possessions in years.
They have forgotten what they have.
They find things they thought they'd lost.
Other things they wish they'd lost.
They recognize in the sprawl
their lives out of control,
and often they are ashamed.

But Marie Kondo waves away
shame and embarrassment.
She laughs again and claps her hands.
"I love mess," she exults.
To ease the language barrier,

she brings a translator,
but for her message of acceptance,
no translation is necessary.

Marie Kondo asks us to handle
each of our objects one by one
and ask, Does this bring me joy?
We keep only what we say yes to.
Everything else will be donated,
sold, or thrown away,
but not before we hold
what we are discarding
and thank it for its service to us.

In Marie Kondo's culture,
objects have lives of their own.
Examining what we have,
we take stock of our lives
and consider those we live with.
By treating our things with respect
at the end of their use to us,
we respect ourselves as well.

Deciding what to keep is only part
of the work. Marie Kondo reveals
how to make maximum use of space.
She shows us clever Japanese ways
of folding clothes so they stand up
in drawers or on shelves. She uses
dividers and boxes to partition storage,
grouping like objects together neatly.

She teaches that there is joy in order
and order in joy. We respect our things
by putting them away after each use.
We let go of what no longer serves us.
We make a space for ourselves
where there was no space before.

BERNADETTE

I was late to marriage,
late to motherhood.
When I met Jamie in New York,
something blossomed in me
that had been dormant.
His jazz club became my hangout,
I dressed up every night
with some place to go.
He was the owner, and I was his girl.

Jamie's mind had layers of learning
like geologic strata.
He was a born teacher,
a shamanistic poet
and spirit guide for many.
His love was like cool water
from a deep well.

Returning home late at night
after he closed the club,
we stepped over passed-out drunks
in the vestibule of his building
and took the rickety, smelly
elevator up to his penthouse
on the eleventh floor.

From the living room,
you could step out on the rooftop
with the city sparkling below you,

but the walls were crumbling,
and the water pressure so low
that if we wanted to bathe,
we ran the bath, took the dog
for a walk around the block,
and came back to a tub
that was only half full.

The apartment had its charms,
particularly in a snowfall
on a cold winter night,
but it was no place to raise a child.
When Jamie lost the lease on the club,
we moved upstate to my hometown.
He was willing to leave the city
to make a life on my terms.

Jamie took to our small town
between lake and mountains.
He started a jazz festival
and developed a local following.
He reinvented himself as a therapist
and college professor,
author of memoirs, a novel, scripts.
Poetry was at the heart of it,
touching everything he did.
As a therapist, he connected
patients to myths and archetypes.
If you cannot see the pattern,
you cannot know what traps you,
or what will set you free.

He had the festival, and I had
my voice students and dance classes.
Music was the living stream
that nourished us. Words fail music,
sometimes love is a sound
that doesn't need words.

Carolyn completed our family,
our darling, doted-on daughter,
without the advantages
and disadvantages of siblings.
Sometimes Jamie was too wise for her.
She didn't want to be seen so well.

I thought Jamie and I would grow
old together. Then he got sick.
Cancer was the inevitable leveler,
bringing us down, down, down,
after seesawing between hope
and doubt, searching for cures,
reading between the lines
of what the doctors said
for what they didn't say.

I was there to support him,
not to make decisions for him.
I trusted him to know
when to stop trying.
For a while he was excited about
an experimental drug trial in Cuba.
He talked about going there
like it was a vacation,

but he didn't qualify.
M.D. Anderson was our last hope.
Looking back, I think it was crazy
to go to Houston in his condition.

He worked hard to finish his book,
between illusion and despair,
glimmers of wisdom, like twinkling
light between dark trees at twilight.
With his great generosity,
he wanted to give what he knew.
He believed in the quest,
the sacred journey. Even today,
when I read his words,
I feel his soft brown eyes
shining on me.

But the day he held that last book
in his hands, so rushed by his publisher
into print, it was marred by misprints,
he laid his palm on the cover,
not opening it, and looked away.

Grief has its own timetable.
It can't be hurried along.
So it was for Carolyn and me.
Jamie was our foundation.
Without him, we were adrift.
We each had to find our way to shore.
Plagued by migraines,
Carolyn missed so much work
she had to quit. I didn't mind
helping her out for a while,
but I couldn't afford it forever.

We grew into our routines.
Carolyn had Ezra, their dog Pete,
and their life in Brooklyn.
I had my mother, aged ninety-four.
She lived half a mile away
in her own house, and every day
I brought her dinner at five o'clock,
alternating with my brother,
who brought her breakfast.
When Jamie was sick, my brother
had taken over. Now it was my turn.

The spring before he died,
Jamie programmed the jazz festival
one last time. It was his memorial:
mid-September, the warm golden sunlight
reflected off the lake, and the horns,
reeds, percussion and strings all glinting
as their melodies rose in the air
played by musicians who'd returned
year after year and become
like family. Sometimes
I imagine an echo still lingers there,
and Jamie is listening.

That was one of the great days
of my life. Afterwards, everything
got darker. Fall led into winter,
and winter into spring with agonizing
slowness. I worried about Carolyn,
how to help her. I was a ghost of myself,
my expression in the mirror so sad

I forced myself to smile. At first
I could only manage a grimace,
but I practiced every day
until it got easier, and I looked better.
When I looked better, I felt better.
You use what you have.

A year after Jamie died, I returned
to a museum we both loved. I stood
before one of Jamie's favorite paintings
and remembered what he'd said about it
as if he were standing next to me.
Tears welled in my eyes. I realized
Jamie is always with me
if only I can look into my heart.

That August was my high school reunion.
I was of two minds,
but I talked myself into it.
On the evening cruise on the lake,
I opened a closed door to my past,
and Bill was there waiting
as if he'd never left.
In fact, he'd come back
after a career in tech in California,
long divorced, with four grown
children living all over the world,
and grandchildren in college,
or starting out on their own.

He was very different from me,
and yet not so very.
We'd never dated,
but we double-dated,
most memorably at our senior prom.
Funny how Bill remembered
what I'd said after the dance
when the four of us went
skinny-dipping in the lake
at two in the morning,

Bill was our class valedictorian.
I'd thought he'd go to Swarthmore
like me, but he changed his mind
and went to Yale for track and field.
He was state champion in the high jump.
I had forgotten how much I admired him.

All that fall we got reacquainted.
He was gentle. He gave me time.
Together we went hiking and biking.
We had fun working out together.
I was in the best shape I'd been in years.
He gave me back a self I had lost.
Every day he came with me
to bring my mother dinner.
He fit into my life and took up
residence in my heart.

When we were together,
it was as if we were teenagers again.
We gossiped about each other's families.

We went on trips to see the farm
where his father was born,
the house where my grandparents
lived when I was growing up.

But the past would mean nothing
if it were just the past.
Experience seasoned us
and made us more tolerant.
When I sometimes call Bill Jamie
in the reflexive way old people have,
he doesn't get upset.
At his embarrassed smile,
I realize what I've said and blush,
but he's already forgiven me.
He gives me room to make mistakes.
What better sign of love is there?
Wherever Jamie's spirit is,
I hope there is no jealousy.

II
SIGNS

SIGNS

A brief April snow disrupted our spring.
Amid clumps of snow, daffodils
nodded in the icy breeze. A glaze
of snowflakes sugared the hyacinths.

I worried for them and the tender lettuces,
red and green, I'd only just planted.
But the sun came out; by mid-morning,
the snow was gone as if it hadn't come.

You'd have to be able to read the signs—
the water drops glistening gaily
on the new leaves, the green moss
wet and velvety, the bushes slick.

Perhaps patience is the key, I thought.
How hard it is to wait out a siege.
The enemy is the invisible virus,
and there is no way out but through.

Once it has passed, we will have to know
where to look to spot the absences
only glaring for those who miss
what has ceased to exist.

LADY BIRD

In my day, women had their sphere,
and men had theirs. I became an observer,
concealing myself behind public duties.
Some people mocked me for my devotion
to wildflowers. Let her occupy herself,
they said, with a cause of little importance,
leaving us free for matters of consequence.

There is a damaged place in each of us.
With me, Lyndon never had to be ashamed
of the gawky farm boy yoked to poverty
as a result of his father's foolish dreams.

I come from a long line of women
who learned to look the other way.
They lived with what they couldn't change.
It didn't mean they liked it. I knew
he'd never risk his career to leave me.
He was a disappointing husband,
but I would never leave him.

There's a reason I love wildflowers.
They're not glamorous or flashy.
They have a modest prettiness
that's worth a second look.
The seeds may lie dormant for years,
settled or buried, blown by the wind,
but one day they will take hold and bloom.
Then they will be everywhere.

DAYS OF 1978

I remember the bad behavior
of the male professors
in my graduate writing program,
how they preyed on young women,
who were predisposed
to hope their teachers
valued their talents
and would help their careers.

Writing is seduction.
Words have a physical body
that comes to life
when wielded by poets.

When intentions are dishonest,
words become weapons,
and everything gets confused,
emotions running
like rainwater in rivulets
trying to find a course
or make one.

THE PROFESSOR'S NECKTIE

One winter nearly a century ago,
Professor G's Massachusetts farmhouse
caught fire and burned down.
He was a gentleman farmer
and lived there only in the summers.

No one knew how the fire started.
It was the depths of the Depression.
Desperate people roamed the countryside.

Notified by a neighbor,
the volunteer fire department arrived
too late to save the house.

Professor and Mrs. G drove up
the next day. Among the ruins
they found a volume
of Robert Frost's poetry.

The cover was warped,
and there were scorch marks
at the edges of the pages.

On the title page still smelling
of smoke was the poet's inscription.
His conventional message conveyed
his good wishes to the professor.

The occasion was a poetry reading
at the college five years ago.
There was a celebratory dinner
for Frost before the reading,
where faculty were invited.

The poet arrived at the last minute
without a necktie, despite
having been given explicit instructions
about the college dress code.

So Frost could attend his own dinner,
Professor G loaned him a beautiful tie
purchased the previous year
from a London haberdasher
made of fine silk in rich stripes
of blue, red, and gold.

Frost wore the tie to dinner
and afterwards to the reading.
When he left the next morning,
he took the tie with him
and never did return it,
although the professor wrote
to remind him it was not a gift.

123 HOME FREE

"The Lord is my Shepherd; I shall not want."
                                        -Psalm 23

I

In the Swiss Alps, once upon
a time, there lived a goatherd
without family as far as anyone knew.
Whenever a window got broken,
or a horse went lame, Peter was
the culprit blamed by the townsfolk.

Peter was happiest with his goats,
climbing rocky paths to alpine meadows.
A glow lingered in the sky behind
the mountain peaks, as the sun slipped
towards the hidden horizon,
and even in July the air turned cold.

Peter called the herd with his horn,
leading them up the mountain by day
and down to safety at night.
The goats, fed on wildflowers,
gave milk that made a delicate cheese.

II

One hundred fifty years later,
Aaron Fletcher lives
off gleanings of the land
in Ashland, Oregon,
with his small flock.

He started with goats
but switched to sheep
for their sweeter milk
and their gift of wool.

He calls himself
"homeless by choice,"
but he has a tiny home
mounted on a bicycle cart.
It looks ramshackle,
yet every inch is planned.

A folding awning protects
the sheep in rainy weather.
There is water storage,
a solar oven, a condensing refrigerator,
a trough of red worms
to compost his waste.
He felts fleece into wool
in a cardboard box
and sews his clothes.
He makes old tires into sandals.

Milk and cheese from his ewes
form the basis of his diet,
supplemented by foraged plants,
dumpster diving, and donations.
He grinds wild seeds for flour
and bakes bread laced with herbs.

His sheep are adoptions or trades.
Their needs determine his daily routine.
He finds them nutritious grasses
and trees with fruits and nuts.
He tends their wounds, guards their health,
and keeps them safe from harm.
In turn, they clothe and feed him.

He calls himself a "community
prepper" with minimal participation
in the market economy
and claims to have found
a way to live off the land
without harming it.

Sometimes he trades work
for the right to shelter
and forage on private property.
Though he talks about his friends,
he always seems to be alone
except for the sheep,
his constant companions.
He knows their personalities
and calls them by name.

People he calls friends allow him
to use their land for grazing
and shelter and give him food,
but they rarely share his company.

Does Aaron represent the vanguard
or the rearguard? With his bristling beard,
unkempt hair, and bushy eyebrows,
he resembles a prophet of old,
his narrow blue eyes glinting
like ice or fire, as he condemns
the hypocrisy of almost everyone,
his speech spiked with obscenity.

But on stony journeys with his sheep
at the highway's edge, under blazing skies,
he croons them wordless songs of comfort.

THE OLD PROFESSOR

I

Forty-five years ago, I showed up
at his office at the scheduled hour
for a makeup map quiz. The shapes
of the mountains and rivers and lakes
of Latin America lay like neural synapses
and pathways across the inner landscape
of my brain as, keyed up and nervous,
I knocked on the door, waited, knocked again.

At last he answered it, visibly startled,
while strains of Bach wafted around him.
He had forgotten our appointment,
and I had interrupted him.
Embarrassed, I apologized,
but no matter: he selected a test
from a stack and disappeared,
leaving me to take it on my own.

I remember the strangeness I felt
at my glimpse into his private life.
I had never thought about what
my teachers did when they were alone.
As I took his test, I wondered,
did I wake him from a nap? His hair
was mussed as if he had been sleeping,
though I might just as well have
summoned him from reading.

Now a professor emeritus,
with the leisure to revisit
his research of fifty years ago,
he finds threads still untied
and uncharted paths to follow.
He has written a new paper
about his old book. It bristles
with footnotes, raising questions
and suggestions. "It's work
I hope I won't live to complete,
or I'd be a hundred and ten.
This legacy I leave to someone else."
His voice barely a whisper,
lost in his own minutiae, deploring:
"I have outlived my hearing,
like so much else."

II

I think of those country people,
fierce and unsmiling,
equipped with rifle and sword,
their chests crisscrossed by bandeliers,
victors and victims in the armed struggles
whose causes he analyzed,
whose legacies he clarified.
Human violence is the constant,
history is told by the winners
or by the losers who keep
memories of their losses alive.

It is the historian's work
to separate myth from reality,
to make meaning from the jumbled past,
to reveal our forebears as they were,
not as we would have them be.

AUDEN'S BOOKCASE

Julian was a book designer
who dealt in antiques on the side.
Two dozen chairs hung from the ceiling
of his one-bedroom apartment
in an East Village tenement.

Arranged on tables and dressers,
gilt and silver picture frames
held daguerreotypes and photos
of someone else's ancestors.
Even the silver was mismatched.

We bought an oak librarian's table,
four oak chairs, and a mahogany
bookcase with glass-fronted shelves.
The table became my desk, the chairs
our dining chairs. We found room
for the bookcase in our bedroom.
It held journals, my jewelry box,
photo albums and scrapbooks.

Julian later moved to Hoboken.
In the eighties, he died of AIDS.
We still have his table and chairs,
but when we moved to a new apartment
after our daughter was born,
there was no room for the bookcase.

I put up a sign in the neighborhood,
advertising it for sale. I received
an inquiry almost immediately.
In the dusk of early evening,
the buyer pressed me over the phone
for a lower price, and I found myself
yielding despite my wish not to.

He arrived right away.
Slender, with dark, curling hair
and rounded shoulders,
he wasted no time with preliminaries.
I was having second thoughts,
but he held me to his bargain.
He was forceful and aggressive,
and I was overwhelmed.

As he dismantled the shelves
to carry them one by one
from the lobby of our building
to his nearby apartment,
an empty envelope fluttered out
from the warped backboard,
four inches by six inches,
the upper left-hand corner
printed with the return address:

"Random House, Inc.
457 Madison Avenue
New York, N. Y. 10022,"

and addressed by hand to:

"Professor W. H. Auden
77 St. Marks Place
New York, N.Y."

There was no stamp,
no postmark, no date.
On the back of the envelope,
under the old Random House logo,
the poet had scribbled a shopping list:

"Cigarettes
Butter
Veg
Sausages"

Around the list was a rectangle,
as if for emphasis.

AT THE POET'S LAST READING

In memory of Mark Strand

In his poems, the drama is elemental:
There was no pain. It had gone.
There were no secrets. There was nothing to say.
The shade scattered its ashes.
The body was yours, but you were not there.
The air shivered against its skin.
The dark leaned into its eyes.
But you were not there.

Those poems light as air
that used to want to fly away
are now trapped between the covers
of a book three inches thick
and hundreds of pages.

Thoughtfully taking in
its heft and size,
the poet balanced the volume
in his open palm, allowing
himself the comment,
"Not bad for a life's work."

I was waiting for him to sign
the copy he was holding.
He didn't notice me at all.
He was looking at the young man
ahead of me about to leave,
as if he were willing

some youthful part of himself
to plant its seed in him
and go forward into
that new life.

        I remember
the moment so clearly,
as if I could actually observe
the flight of one soul
into another, and the youth,
radiating his own glow,
unsuspecting.

        The poet
was lean as a razor,
his once-handsome features
craggy as a rock face.
I thought "ill," but not
"dying." Yet in two months
he was dead.

FROM THE LIFE OF IRIS ORIGO

(a cento, mostly)

"The days go by waiting for better times."

I

Day after day we sat in the library
of our isolated country house,
listening to the voices on the radio
with an increasing sense of doom —
Hitler and Dolfuss, Eden and Chamberlain,
schoolchildren and soldiers singing Fascist anthems.

On June 10, 1940, we were ordered
to listen to Il Duce's speech.
We set up our radio in our courtyard
where a hundred people gathered,
who lived in the local villages
or were tenants on our estate.

In the long delay before the broadcast,
Antonio and the keeper
discussed the young partridges
and twin calves born that morning.
The keeper said one wouldn't live.

Mussolini's speech was pompous,
bombastic, and full of lies,
the gist being that Italy was at war
with England and France. Afterwards,
people shuffled away in silence.

We stood looking at each other—
Italian husband and English wife.
"Ci siamo," said Antonio.
"I'm going to inspect the wheat."
Gloomily, we fetched our hats and coats.

II

At seven she lost
her beloved American father
who died of TB at thirty.
At seven, her only son
succumbed to meningitis.

These losses defined her life
with the negative space
of their cancelled lives
and her unfulfilled longings.

III

As a fatherless child, she was feuded over
by her American and English grandparents,
but they were defeated by her father's dying wish
that she be raised without a national identity.

At nine, her artistic mother moved them to Fiesole,
where she spent a lonely, fairy tale youth
in the magnificent villa designed by Michelozzo
for Cosimo di Medici, with its terraces and gardens

restored by her mother with her father's wealth.
Raised in a hothouse atmosphere of intellectual
expatriates, tending to her invalid mother
or accompanying her on journeys in quest of culture,

she found solace in books and could read
three languages by the age of six. "*Although
any language will do for telling a story, some things
are better said in one language than in another.*"

Her happiest hours were spent as the private pupil
of Solone Monti, who decided to try out on her
the Humanist education Vittorino da Feltre
gave Cecilia Gonzaga in the fifteenth century,

in which Greek and Latin were learned together,
as living languages, and poetry was considered
the fittest instrument to train the mind.
Without school syllabi and exams,

her mind was free to roam. Say it in any
language you like, said Monti, but feel the poetry.
The path of learning was enlivened
and made easier by elements of surprise.

"*For nearly three years, from ages twelve to fifteen,
my imagination was entirely filled by the world
he conjured up for me, and I owe him
not only what he taught me then,*

but, in enthusiasm and method of approach,
all that I have learned ever since." In 1917,
Monti died of the Spanish flu. Her dreams
of Oxford were quashed by her mother,

who insisted she 'come out' as a debutante
in three countries. In New York and London,
she was clueless and miserable. "*The only dance*
I enjoyed was the one my mother gave me

at Villa Medici on a moonlit night in June.
I had a ball gown from a couturier
in shades of blue and silver shoes,
and I almost felt pretty. The terrace,

where supper was laid on little tables,
was lit with Japanese lanterns. Fireflies
darted among the darkened wheat
in the farm below, and the air

was perfumed with roses and jasmine.
At midnight, fireworks from the terrace
soared like jeweled fountains
between us and the valley."

IV

Although it is necessary, sooner or later,
to learn something of the ways of the world,
I would have been happier at Oxford,
working at subjects I cared about,

instead of exposed to values I did not share,
but was not yet brave enough to disregard.
I encouraged men whom I did not like
and was distressed when they fell in love.

At eighteen I met my future husband
chaperoning his younger sister at a dance.
Two years later, when we met again,
he was caring for his father dying of cancer.

After long nights at his father's bedside,
he would walk up the Fiesole hill
to meet me in the early morning.
Eventually we reached an understanding.

In marrying Antonio, I chose life in Italy
over England or America. We bought
a large, neglected estate in southern Tuscany,
seeking a pastoral, productive existence.

Of life's pleasures, only books and reading,
at every age, have never failed me,
but in the early years of my marriage,
I stopped writing, bound up with the farm,

my son, and my husband's interests. Only
after Gianni's death did I return to writing.
Seeking impersonal work to absorb my thoughts
and distract my grief, I chose biography.

Might I, who always preferred
being an observer to being observed,
assemble the parts of someone else's life
and character into a pattern?

The only tribute the biographer can pay
to his subject is to tell the truth.
But what is the truth about any of us?
A record of happenings is not a life.

There are facts about ourselves
we do not tell or do not know.
The biographer must seize the small facet
of truth that catches the light.

The biographer's real work
is to bring the dead to life
in the context of the universal drama.
George Santayana, my father's teacher,

wrote to me after Gianni died,
"All our affections, when
not claims to possession,
transport us to another world,

and the loss of contact, here or there,
with those eternal beings,
is like closing a book which we keep
at hand for another occasion."

DANTE'S TOMBS

I

Seven hundred years ago,
Dante died in exile in Ravenna
and was buried there.

His native Florence
refused his body,
but two centuries later,
Florence wanted him back.

The Pope approved the transfer,
but the monks in Ravenna
returned an empty coffin
to Florence's new memorial.

They had removed the poet's bones
from his tomb for safekeeping
and interred them in the basilica wall

where they lay forgotten
for three hundred years,
until a renovation revealed them,

and they were buried
in a mausoleum near the church
on a side street so narrow
it is easy to miss.

Forty years ago we visited Ravenna
and found Dante's tomb,
the worn white marble
softened by lichens,
the inscription so weathered
it was hard to read.

How modest it seemed
after a day of monuments
already ancient in Dante's time,
Justinian's mosaics in blue and gold
and the tomb of Gallia Placida
that inspired *Purgatorio* and *Paradiso*.

Once the western outpost
of a great empire, today's
Ravenna is a backwater,
surrounded by marshes
dotted with oil wells.

II

One hundred years ago,
after the Great War,
an Italian immigrant to Argentina

resolved to build Dante
a worthy monument
in his new country
on the other side of the world,

a building emerging
from the depths of the earth
reaching to the heavens,

in every detail and at every level
an embodiment
of Dante's great poem,

elaborate and fantastical,
a celebration of the imaginary
over the mundane,

realized as a skyscraper
named for himself,
the Palacio Barolo.

Twenty-two floors representing
twenty-two stanzas
sit on a foundation
scaled to the golden ratio.

The visitor begins in hell,
progresses to purgatory,
and ascends to heaven.

The lobby, crowned
with Latin inscriptions
and statues of serpents,
dragons, and condors,

radiates from a central dome
into nine vaulted archways,
the nine circles of hell,

lit by red lights
set in metal flowers.

Geometric patterns
representing alchemist's fire
and Masonic symbols
decorate floors, ceilings,
and elevator walls
in red, white, and green tiles,
the colors of the Italian flag.

The higher levels,
corresponding to heaven,
begin at an observation deck
overlooking the sprawl
of Buenos Aires,

crowned by a lighthouse
at the highest point
of one hundred meters,
like the Divine Comedy's
one hundred Cantos,
topped by a statue of Dante
ascending to heaven.

Architect Pilanti intended
the light from the tower
of the Palacio Barolo
to cross the light
from the Palacio Salvo,
his sister building across
the Rio de la Plata
in Montevideo,

the two beams mingling
like the heavenly union
of Dante and Beatrice,
welcoming visitors
to the great estuary
like the Pillars of Hercules
to the Mediterranean.

By a miscalculation
of the earth's curvature,
the beams never crossed,
and the cupola, intended
for Dante's remains,
remains empty.

III
AN ART STORY

AN ART STORY

Part One: The Gallery

An art book about depictions of animals
in antique furniture led me to a gallery
on a side street of the Upper East Side,
its façade shaded by a graceful street tree.
Inside were three floors of treasures.
It was a store without price tags,
attracting a certain class of clientele.

I was not one of them. Yet I was greeted
by the proprietor, a willowy woman
with ash-blond hair, "of a certain age,"
casually elegant in tweed skirt and sweater.
Sometimes a perfect stranger will open up to me,
and so it was that day for Elena and me.

She'd put her trust in a young man,
her daughter's Harvard classmate,
with beautiful manners and clothes.
He impressed her with his knowledge
of art and antiques and promise
of access to rich, young customers.

After he graduated from college,
she hired him. His salary was low,
but he lived rent-free above the gallery,
with an expense account larger
than his pay. He was given shares

in the business after years of service
and managed the gallery's finances.

The trouble began when he wanted her
to buy him out. She discovered
art and objects had gone missing,
and there was far less money
than there should have been.

It was the oldest trick in the book,
a vulnerable older woman taken
advantage of by a younger man.
As I expressed my sympathy,
I felt a mix of pity and scorn
at how she'd been taken in.

A year later I went to an opening
and saw her from across the room.
Sometimes I would glimpse the gallery
through the window of an uptown bus,
or walk by on my way to another destination,
but I didn't go back.

Part Two: The Nemi Ships

Two thousand years ago,
the Emperor Caligula
commissioned two ships
of immense beauty
and spectacular luxury.
Although seaworthy,
they never went to sea,

but were moored in Lake Nemi,
a volcanic crater of clear water,
dedicated to the goddess Diana
in the Alban Hills south of Rome.

In the galley ship was a temple
for the worship of the goddess,
granting it religious exemption
from Roman law forbidding
boats on the sacred lake.
Inside the temple,
a marble statue of Diana
revolved on a wooden turntable
mounted on bronze spheres.

The second ship was a floating palace
with sumptuous rooms
and shaded terraces, marble baths
with piped hot and cold water,
fruit-bearing trees in pots,
statues in niches,
and mosaic pavements
of green and red porphyry
and serpentine
and molded glass
in geometric patterns.

When the fiery eye of the sun
put itself out in the liquid dark,
the ship was transformed
into a vehicle of pleasure
when pleasure meant excess.

The ships were sunk
after Caligula's assassination
or in the following decades,
and lay submerged
at the bottom of Lake Nemi,
under sixty feet of water,
but their historical memory persisted,
passed down through generations.

Alberti, in the Renaissance,
tried to retrieve the pleasure ship
with iron hooks attached
to the hull by swimmers,
but the hooks ripped apart the hull.

In 1827 eight men descended
in Fusconi's diving bell.
They pulled timbers from the hull
that were carved into curios
and collected architectural details
and artifacts that were sold for profit.

From the second ship,
located seventy years later,
came the astonishing bronzes
in Rome's Terme museum.

Mussolini's great triumph
was the draining of the lake
with massive electric turbines
through an ancient Roman conduit.
The pleasure boat was retrieved in 1929

and the galley temple in 1932.
They were larger, more elaborate,
and technologically advanced
than anyone had dreamed,
and perfectly preserved
from their centuries' long immersion.

Removed from the protection
of the sacred waters,
they deteriorated in the open air.
A museum was built to shelter them,
but fifteen years after they were salvaged,
Caligula's ships were destroyed.
German soldiers fleeing the Allies
in 1944 set the museum on fire
in a calculated act of arson.

The blaze reduced the wooden ships
to ashes, leaving fragments of brick,
charred stone and terracotta,
and thousands of copper nails.

The only surviving objects
were the artifacts acquired
by the Terme museum
in the last century—
the decorative bronze heads
of lions, wolves, and panthers
that gripped the mooring rings
and capped the oars, fragments
of surface decoration,
a square of a tessellated pavement

in a geometric pattern
of white glass and marble
and red and green porphyry.

After the Second World War,
the mosaic left the museum.
No one could say what happened.

Part Three: The Connoisseurs

As a young man, the future
lapidary expert Mario Guardelli
had an eye for colored stone
and a special love of porphyry.
In an art gallery in Rome in the 1960s,
he saw Caligula's mosaic on display
and snapped a picture. Then it went missing.
Decades later, he included the photo
in his book about imperial decoration
and red and purple as emblems of power.

At Guardelli's book party in New York,
a guest, leafing through the pages,
stopped when he saw the photo.
"That's Elena's mosaic," he exclaimed,
as other guests gathered around.
It seemed they all had seen it.
"Who is Elena?" Guardelli asked,
and was told, "She's a woman
who lives on Park Avenue,
and this mosaic is her coffee table."

An Italian art official at the party
overheard the conversation
and alerted the New York authorities.
They started an investigation,
and four years later seized the table.

The shock when the police entered
her apartment with a search warrant
nearly gave Elena a heart attack—
 "It was as if I were a smuggler or a thief.
My husband bought the mosaic
from an aristocratic family.
When it arrived in New York,
we had it attached to a marble frame
and mounted on a pedestal.
We used it as a coffee table.
We had it 45 years.
We never tried to hide it."

Elena said she could not recall
the seller's name,
or how much they paid,
nor could she produce a bill of sale.
She agreed to relinquish the mosaic,
and was not charged with any crime.
"To disregard the provenance
of an art purchase is to give
tacit approval to criminal practice,"
commented the New York district attorney.
"Good title cannot be passed
on a stolen object."

How did the mosaic come
into possession of the family that sold it?
Elena couldn't or wouldn't say.
Her husband, Luigi Corsini,
was a well-known journalist
and a Florentine count. Elena claimed
that the sale of an object of antiquity
by a noble family, brokered by a friend,
was typical among their acquaintance.

They were like the collectors in the last centuries
who carved walking canes and smoking pipes
from the timbers of Caligula's ship,
when they converted their fragment
of his ship's pavement to a coffee table.
Year after year, they set down on it
their mugs of coffee and tea, their glasses of wine,
their candlesticks and their vases of flowers.
It was their hearth, the center of their home.

It distressed Elena to lose her table.
It was a link to life with her husband,
mourned for twenty years,
but she had no means to fight the seizure.
No matter what they knew or did not know,
she and her husband had skirted the rules.
The mosaic had come to New York
from Italy smuggled without papers
by diplomatic pouch.

The Italian restorers took four years
to eradicate the wine and coffee stains

before the mosaic went on display
in the National Museum.
If you look closely at the mosaic
now in its place of honor,
you can discern the faint,
white ring of a calcium stain
left by a vase of water,
like a ghost.

Part Four: The Rebirth

Gerald Lathrop speaks:

My mother loved words.
Poetry was her medium.
Words stick in my throat
and get trapped in my mouth.
I put my love into things.
Art and furniture.
Rooms and windows.
Rugs and fabrics and porcelains.
Life on the surface
has always appealed to me,
if the surface is beautiful.

I intended to become a new person
when I went east to Harvard.
I took her name and gave up his.
I didn't talk about my past.
I applied myself to decoration,
the art of making things look
better than they are.

I cultivated an appearance.
Appearances can be deceiving.

When I met Patricia,
I felt right away that she
was who I wanted to be,
if I were female. We
misunderstood the attraction
at first. We were better siblings
than lovers. I needed a family,
and I fit right into the slot
where a brother would go.
Her parents welcomed me,
and her home became my home.
That very first Christmas I spent
with them in Italy. My sisters
said they would miss me,
but they had already made
their own separate lives,
and wherever *he* was,
it was not my home.

Don't think I didn't know
that the Corsinis liked me
to be attractive and attentive.
I was like a mirror,
reflecting back what I saw.
The reflection kept me
from looking inward.

It was understood I would go
to work for them when I graduated.

They made me a rent-free apartment
above the gallery and paid the tuition
for my master's degree in art history.
At their expense I dressed well,
I went out all the time. I traveled
to Europe on gallery business.
They did everything but give me
a decent salary. I felt safe
among the art and antiques,
as if their presence were protection,
as far away from my past as I could get.

I enjoyed working with customers,
leading them to treasures
they might not have noticed.
When the silence in the shop
grew oppressive, I got a little dog.
I stood next to Patricia when
she married *her* Italian count.

The Corsinis had a roundabout
way of operating. In Italy, it seems,
it is a way of life to skirt the rules.
I adapted. We supported each other.
I was happy enough living
with old, beautiful things,
or thought I was.

But all the while there was
buried fear and anger,
like poison vapors trapped inside
an abandoned mine, waiting to explode.

Because no matter how far away
I got in time and space,
a part of me never left
that rainy, foggy California night
my senior year in high school
when I came home very late
after a Saturday night with friends
to find two policemen waiting for me
to tell me my mother was dead
from a shotgun blast,
and the shooter was my father.

It was his antique gun.
Dad was in the Marines
in Vietnam, and he collected guns.
He said he showed it to my mother
when he was cleaning it, and it went off
and shot her in the chest.
He convinced the police
it was a tragic accident.
But we never believed him.
Not me, or my sisters,
or my Uncle Andy.

Mom was afraid of Dad,
and she didn't like guns.
She'd been sleeping in the room
above the garage.
They both had lovers.
She was planning to leave him
when I went to college.

Sometimes I wonder if Hamlet
really saw his father in supernatural aspect
or if the ghost was a figment of his mind.
I was hiking in the Olympic peninsula,
when I thought I saw my mother
walking ahead of me through the fog
between two ancient spruce trees.
Though I saw her from the back,
I recognized her by the square set
of her slim shoulders and the way
she walked on the balls of her feet,
like a dancer. She tossed her head
the way Mom used to do,
and a shiver went through me.
I was afraid she would turn around.
I didn't want to see the wounds
that blossomed on her chest.
I hid behind a tree, closed my eyes,
and stopped up my ears
until she was gone. Afterwards,
I was ashamed of myself.

Dad's girlfriend moved into our house
right after Mom died. Dad promised
to pay tuition for me and my sisters,
but he didn't. Uncle Andy took over.
He paid the bills for our education
and hired an attorney and a detective.
Thirteen years after Mom's death,
a police agent determined
from the forensic evidence
that she was kneeling with her arms

shielding her face when she was killed,
vainly trying to protect herself
from the blow she feared was coming.
A grand jury indicted my father,
and he was arrested, tried, convicted,
and sentenced to life in prison.

I went to see him in the county jail
before the trial, and that was it.
I don't know where he's serving now.
I cut him out of my life.
When he went to prison,
something in me was liberated.
I realized I'd been afraid of him.
In some sense I'd barricaded myself
in the gallery, and now I was free to go.

A month later I met Terence Ingram
at The Winter Show for Art and Antiques.
He's an interior designer. I loved his exhibit.
He invited me to his studio, and we went
for a drink. We knew right away.
Everything meshed between us.
By then Luigi had died, and Patricia
was married and living in Italy.
I expected some difficulty
when I told Elena about Terence,
but not what happened.

I asked Elena for a reasonable salary
Instead, she doubled my expense account.
It wouldn't do. In my letter of resignation,

I thanked her for all she'd done,
told her I'd moved out of her apartment,
and asked her to buy back the gallery shares
Luigi left me in his will. When I returned
to the apartment to get the rest of my things,
she'd changed the locks. After that,
it just got worse.

The phrase, "a fine Italian hand,"
defined a style of penmanship
that replaced Gothic script
in the seventeenth century.
It came to refer to a skill
or expertise. To me it also suggests
a process that is hidden or concealed,
hence "underhanded."
I think of "a fine Italian hand,"
when I think of Elena,
her exquisite refinement
and her sneaky, circuitous ways.

The buying and selling of antiquities
has always been a shady business.
Beautiful things arouse ugly vices.
In Italy, avoiding taxation
is a national sport. These principles,
applied in America, yielded profits shared
with clients all too willing to comply.
Elena taught me her way of doing business
and left me in charge while she went off
to restore her castle on her Tuscan hilltop.
When she denied me commissions

and raises, I took what I felt entitled to
and justified to myself what I did.
As a precaution, I photocopied records
of the gallery's transactions, arming myself
with evidence of her misdeeds.

When she failed to respond
to my requests, I filed a lawsuit.
She countersued, accusing me of theft.
Early one fall morning a year later,
as Terence and I lay sleeping,
we were startled awake by banging
and yelling: "Police!" In his bathrobe,
Terence opened the door
to eight officers, guns drawn,
brandishing a search warrant.
I was naked, and they watched me dress.
They marched me through the lobby
while neighbors watched,
and took me to the new gallery
I had opened with Terence,
where more policemen waited.

That was the end of Elena in my life.
She was trying to put me in jail.
Naturally, Patricia took her mother's side.
I felt my whole life come crashing down.
It was even worse than
when my mother was killed.

I was accused of stealing
35 works of art and 300 art books

and incurring expenses
beyond what I was allowed.
The charge was grand larceny,
embezzlement, and criminal
possession of stolen property
valued at one-half million dollars.
They seized Patricia's paintings
she had given to me and books
inscribed to me by my professors.
If convicted, I faced up to 15 years.
In return for a reduced sentence,
I cooperated with investigators.
Elena's business methods came back
to bite her. I was sentenced
to three years' probation
and had to pay $57,000,
representing 12 years of taxes
I'd never declared
on the rent-free apartment
and expense account,
and the sales taxes I'd evaded
on purchases from the gallery.
Elena's tab was much larger:
$675,000 in back taxes and fines.

I had proof of the many occasions
she avoided paying sales taxes
by creating false shipment records,
mailing catalogues to out-of-state addresses,
while sending the actual purchases
to New York residences.
She had no choice but to plead

guilty to tax evasion. Our dispute
over my shares in the gallery
and objects that she said were stolen,
and I claimed were gifts, ended
in an unsatisfactory compromise.

With Terence, I have the life
I aspired to. My work is more
than business; it's an obsession.
I like to create settings,
where I put together objects
of different styles and ages
so they engage in a conversation,
and an odd, unloved piece,
revealed in a new context,
may finally be appreciated.

Part Five: The Thing Itself

Elena Corsini speaks:

Regret has a bitter taste.
For 45 years the mosaic
was mine, and no one
can take that away.
My life was about acquiring,
now I have to let go.

It is said Caligula built
a third floating palace
to complete his fleet.
It, too, was sunk after his death

and lies so deep in the mud
at the bottom of Lake Nemi
it has never been found.
From time to time, there is talk
of mounting a new search.
Like so much in Italy,
it gets put off. If the ship exists,
I hope it is never found.

SURREALIST MUSE

The sense of a vessel is not in its shell, but in its void.
—Dag Hammarskjold

Loplop imagined a beguiling woman-child
whose purpose was to inspire him,
not to understand him.
She was meant to be his destiny,
sparking his creativity, leading him to visions,
a mirror in which he saw himself.

"*Who is the Bride of the Wind?*" he sang.
"*She cannot read or write without mistakes,
but she warms herself with her intense love,
her mystery, her poetry.*"

They shared a belief that art is alchemy.
Loplop was a blue-eyed bird
with fierce talons and soft feathers,
and Leonora was a white horse
with a mane of long hair
and the power of flight.

He made her the instrument of his passion,
and she loved him for it anyway.
In an old stone house near a river
of deep gorges and limestone cliffs,
and stones polished to a high gloss
by the river's rough bottom,
he nourished her painting and poetry.

The mythic and occult
Leonora had sought since childhood
came to dwell with them
for a year of days filled with light
falling through the open shutters
of the tall windows of the studio
where she painted mysterious images
with enigmatic meanings
and cooked exotic dishes in a rustic kitchen,
and he decorated house and garden
with sculptures of mythical creatures.

"For two years I've been madly in love.
I'm painting only to keep from going crazy.
I want him to live only for me.
I wish that he had no past.
I want us to be in the same body.
Absolute love, I want him forever."

This was in Saint-Martin-d'Ardeche,
in the south of France before the war,
before he was imprisoned as an enemy alien,
and she was left alone with their five cats
in the house she now called "The House of Fear:"

"Without you, I am losing my sense of life,
of everything I owe to knowing you.
In despair, I bite my fingers violently;
my body has changed into an animal."

His release at Christmas was a reprieve.
In the new year he painted her portrait

in the dawn light of a tropical landscape.
In May he was denounced and arrested again,
and sent to a prison farther away.
Coerced into giving away the house,
she fled with friends, leaving their creations
and possessions behind.

She struggled to find a way forward.
The car jammed, and she was jammed.
The road of escape was lined with death.
She felt herself absorbing the world's ills,
her consciousness leaking from her body.
Craving deliverance, she was betrayed
and abandoned by everyone
from whom she sought protection.

Abducted in Madrid, raped, and stripped
of her clothes and identification papers,
she left body and soul behind,
escaping into the shamanic visions
of an alchemist with the fantastic touch
of a fairy tale wizard,
invoking images and enigmas
with no solution in reason,
like the erotic dream-worlds
conjured in ceremonies
of ancient feminine cults.

"I tried to empty myself of the images
that had made me blind.
Armed with madness for a long voyage,
I wandered into the unknown
with the abandon and courage of ignorance."

Confined to a mental institution
in the north of Spain,
shackled naked to a bed,
her skin ravaged by mosquitoes,
lying in feces, sweat, and urine,
treated with drugs that gave her convulsions,
she was plunged into the depths.

"At the bottom of the well
was the stopping of my mind
for all eternity in utter anguish.
I entered a state of prostration,
and when I awoke, I regained my lucidity.
The next day I met a small man
with a gray face who told me,
'Power over animals is a natural thing
in a person as sensitive as you are.'"

Loplop once said, "*To create the fantastic,*
you must use the banal."
Through luck, chance, and cunning,
she managed a series of escapes.
After a year apart and an anguished search,
he located her in Lisbon.

She was living under the protection
of the Mexican ambassador,
who offered her a way out of Europe,
the war, and the long reach
of her oppressive family,
who intended to commit her
to an asylum in South Africa.

Loplop, too, had found a sponsor,
an American heiress with an art collection,
who'd fallen in love with the artist
as well as the art.

If only Leonora had stayed in Saint-Martin,
he might not have lost her
or the house on the cliffs.
Thanks to the French wife he'd abandoned,
he was released soon after Leonora fled.
It was a shock when he returned
to find her missing and her cryptic note,
the house and their belongings
swindled by the innkeeper
he'd thought was their friend.

One moonless night
he broke into the house
and fled with their paintings
by canoe across the river.
The paintings were with him
the next spring when
he found her in Lisbon.

The longed-for reunion was a fiasco.
"Once again my life is a mess,"
he wrote their best friend, Leonor.
"I have found (and lost) Leonora.
She has been crushed, and there is only
an occasional glimpse of her old spirit."

Yet, just a few days later, he wrote again,
"Everything has changed.
Leonora's horrors have ended.
She has become beautiful, vibrant;
it's a miracle."

Through their marriages of convenience,
they both moved to New York,
where he would have left the heiress
for her in a heartbeat, but she refused.
"I was not the same person after Madrid.
There was no way for me to go back."

He gave her his portrait of her
painted in the halcyon months
between his imprisonments,
when he should have made plans to leave,
but persisted instead in a dreamlike bubble,
pretending they could shut out the world,
that led them to disaster.

She gave him the early self-portrait
that had come with her from London
to Paris in the early days of their love,
and he had rescued from the house on the cliff.
In riding clothes and high heels,
she sits in a chair under a rocking horse,
with her mane of dark hair,
as she wards off an evil-eyed hyena
with the sign of the horn, and outside
the window is a fleeing white horse.

She also gave him the portrait
she had made of him as Bird Superior
wearing a pelt of rose-colored feathers
that ends in a forked tail
like the tail of his Maremaid.

Inside the lantern he holds in his delicate hand
shines the image of a white horse.
The white horse that soared across the lawn
is now an eyeless ice sculpture,
frozen to the ground.

One night while she lay sleeping,
he painted over one of her canvases,
then convinced her the next morning
that the painting never existed.
It amused him to play mind-games with her.
She was the youngest of their group,
wearing long skirts and lacy blouses
bought for her in thrift shops.
She went along with their wishes,
until she no longer recognized who she was.

Yet she was "*magnificent in her refusals*,"
said Breton the patriarch, czar of Surrealism.
She said "*No*" to Man Ray taking her picture,
 "*No*" to Miró's request to buy him cigarettes,
"*No*" to Loplop's last entreaties of love.
She said "*No*" to the lot of them,
asking her for this or that,
just as she'd said to her father,
"*No, I will not be who you want me to be,*

or marry who you want," and he'd replied,
"*You will not darken my doorstep again.*"

She might paint her feet with mustard,
snip human hair into an omelet,
shower fully clothed and come out dripping
to sit down among the others,
invite random guests to dinner
from a phonebook. With women friends,
she practiced the occult as culinary art.
The kitchen was her seat of power.

What saved her was her sensitivity
to the natural world, seen and unseen.
"*I could draw near animals*
where other human beings
put them to precipitate flight."

After a year and a half in New York,
she left on a road trip for Mexico
with her ambassador husband
and never saw Loplop again.
Rarely did she speak of him,
but she kept his portrait of her
in her bedroom until the day she died.

Their marriages of convenience soon ended.
Leonora and Loplop found new loves
that lasted the rest of their lives. Dorothea
was an art student from Illinois
when she met Loplop in New York,
and he left the heiress for good to live
with her in Arizona in a house of their art.

Chiki was Leonora's fellow refugee,
a Hungarian-Jewish photographer
who saved thousands of images
from the Spanish Civil War by entrusting
the negatives to a Mexican diplomat
who took them home to his country,
where they were forgotten for fifty years
and then found in his battered leather suitcase.

Chiki and Leonora shared a war-torn past
that found safe haven in Mexico,
where they made a home, raised two sons,
and practiced their arts. Tender and gentle,
Chiki was Leonora's ally in occult explorations.
Although she occasionally visited France,
she never went back to the house on the cliff.

In Mexico she found her spiritual country.
Mystery, darkness, witchcraft—the deep worlds
that she'd always sensed were hidden
existed in plain view under the blazing sun,
amid exotic animals and luxuriant foliage.
Her art responded in a shimmer of secrets,
rendered in translucent egg tempera
she produced in her kitchen.

She wasn't anyone's plaything anymore.
Bitter experience had taught her
how to protect herself. Once, hoping
to seduce her, the filmmaker Buñuel
locked her in his bathroom.
She decorated the walls with handprints
of her menstrual blood.

She claimed a legacy of ancient knowledge,
passed on through generations of women.
She could bring on illness or exorcise it,
provoke dreams in others as their spiritual guide.
A Zen master said of her at fifty,
*"She doesn't know any koans,
but she has resolved them all."*

Her paintings reveal the mysterious beings
that hover close in childhood,
creatures that scurry up and down the spine,
through a net of nerves,
holding torches that cast flickering shadows
into forgotten spaces, through the thin veils
separating this world from the next.

In old age she asserted her right to be a crone:
*"Art is not hereditary. It comes from somewhere else.
If you try to intellectualize it,
you are wasting your time.
You understand through your feelings.
Canvas is an empty space,
and what we see as space changes all the time.
A transparent egg that emits rays
like the great constellations is a body,
but it is also a box."*

ESCAPING LEE MILLER

Luck is stepping out on a limb and sawing it off behind you.
—Lee Miller

Lee Miller had a thing for bondage
as long as she had a say in it.
It was a game, like a feat of Houdini,
to see what she could escape.
The Surrealists were all for games
to augment reality, or while it away,
or transform it. The element
of transgression, of danger,
acted on them like an aphrodisiac.

Lee Miller was good at getting out
of things she didn't want. As a girl,
she got kicked out of every school
her parents sent her. At seventeen,
she sprung out of Poughkeepsie
and landed in Paris, where she got rid
of her chaperone and lived on her own.

In Poughkeepsie again, she fled to New York.
Then Paris, New York, Paris, New York, Egypt.
No place could hold her, and no one could keep her.
She was charming, and she was infuriating,
because even as she escaped, she stayed attached.

In the twenties, in Paris, when she was nineteen
and beautiful, she sought out Man Ray
as the teacher to enable her transition
from model to photographer.

In return for intimacy, she got
the undivided attention of a master.
Man taught Lee everything he knew,
and she was smart and talented enough
to appreciate his investment and come out ahead.

They liked to walk the streets of Paris
tethered to each other by a golden chain,
he leading and she following,
always with a space between them.
She let people assume he was in charge,
but when he became too possessive, she left him.

Whenever things started to get comfortable,
she'd stir them up. It was a quality
she had in common with Picasso—
both of them egotists and narcissists.
Picasso tried but failed to get the better of her.
Man Ray, Picasso, Max Ernst,
even Roland Penrose, the Quaker pacifist
who would become her second husband
and the father of her only child,
all claimed to love women
yet nurtured desires of mutilating
and destroying them. For proof,
just look at what they did
to the women in their art.

Lee overlooked it. She had to,
if she were to join men as equals
and claim their rights and freedoms.
Drink was no big deal; sex was no big deal.

Some women idolized her; others resented her,
because she acted as if she were exceptional,
and the codes other women abided by
didn't apply to her. She got away with it.
She was careless, entitled, and selfish,
fun-loving, impulsive, and daring.
Her life was an adventure,
and her beauty was her currency,
recognized everywhere.

Some of the antics were light-hearted—
driving topless to the beach on the Côte d'Azur,
dancing at night without pants
in the headlights of a car.

Yet, in some of her photographs
images of violence exist uneasily.
Like a meat pie, a severed breast
from a mastectomy is presented on a plate
with silverware, napkin, and glass.

In one of Man's photos, Lee kneels, baring her teeth
and snarling like a wild animal.
Around her neck is a heavy spiked metal collar
attached to a chain held by a scowling man.
It's like a collar used to restrain a beast.
The man? William Seabrook, now forgotten,
who claimed to be a cannibal, and was known
to keep a naked servant girl in his Paris hotel room
and make her eat off the floor.

These pictures are jokes, shocks, warnings.
Lee's boldest actions were results of instinct.
Boredom and restlessness made her a nomad.
In the Depression, she left Paris for New York
and founded a top photography studio.
At the height of success, she married
a wealthy Egyptian and moved to Cairo.

She thought she wanted relief from the need
to take pictures, but she was lured
by the barren landscape and its ancient structures.
While Aziz labored to bring air-conditioning to Egypt,
she trekked through the desert with friends.

From the beginning, the marriage was a mistake.
Like Man, Aziz was old enough to be her father,
and he loved her with a gentle, paternal love,
indulging her and desiring her happiness
at the expense of his own. For no matter
how free Lee claimed to be,
she wanted a father to protect her.

She found Egypt stifling in the colonial thirties.
For a while, desert adventures diverted her,
but soon she was off to Europe in a brand-new car,
bankrolled by her husband. Paris was an oasis
after a long drought. On her first night back,
she showed up at a party, an image of elegance
in a white silk gown, and met Roland Penrose,
stained with blue paint. The two were inseparable.
Seeking freedom in bondage, together
they found release from their secret desires.

In his student days, Roland was a lover of men.
He'd grown up in a strict Quaker household,
and he was tormented. For him to have sex
with a woman, her hands must be tied.
His first wife, Valentine, was a lesbian,
with a vagina too small for him to penetrate.
She objected when he bound her to a tree.

Lee was willing to go along with Roland's fetishes,
confident his bonds couldn't hold her.
Returning to her husband, she pledged to Roland:
It's cold in the train—I'm alone with the noise—
And my years, unlike your chains
--bind me—
it was true—it is true
--I'm leaving—I love you
and I'll return

The next year Lee traveled with Roland
in Greece and Romania. They climbed mountains,
visited temples of the gods, and danced with gypsies.
He followed her to Egypt and reached her in the desert,
where he gave her his book of their travels
and a pair of handcuffs made from gold, signed Cartier.

She claimed to be ecstatic with his gifts
and wore the handcuffs on one wrist
as a bracelet, ever ready to bind both wrists
to fulfill his desire. One night,
attempting an escape while drunk,
she snapped the link. Years later,
the broken handcuffs were stolen.

The hostility of the Surrealist men towards women
is linked to their shameful love of men.
They couldn't acknowledge their mutual desires.
The closest they came to sex with each other
was to share their women. They called it *homage.*
The women went along with their husbands' wishes,
but few of the relationships lasted.

Many men were in love with Lee,
but none she was willing to trust.
On any given day, she might look like a goddess,
a flapper, or the girl next door,
brimming with health and good spirits,
but a wound inflicted in childhood had never healed.
Only her parents and brothers knew.
It was a secret she carried to her grave.

While visiting family friends in Brooklyn
when she was seven years old,
Lee was raped by their nephew
and infected with gonorrhea
which then had no cure. Lee's mother,
a nurse, administered painful
invasive treatments every day for a year.
Lee's screams filled the house.
Her rages dominated the family's moods.
Out of pity and guilt, her wishes were indulged.
The rape was never mentioned,
but knowledge of it underlay everything.

She had been a carefree tomboy,
cross-country skiing and playing ball

with her father and brothers.
Overnight, she became uncontrollable.
Suffering, she took a grim satisfaction
in making others suffer.
Turning order into chaos felt powerful.

But she wasn't only destructive.
Though impatient with academics,
she was clever and picked up skills easily.
Her favorite possession was her chemistry set.
She was a problem solver
and liked tinkering with tools.
She took after her father.
She was his favorite child, and he loved her
with an all-consuming love.

The first photographer in Lee's life
was not Man, but her father.
Theodore liked to photograph his daughter nude,
outdoors or in his basement studio.
Through the double lens of the stereopticon,
two images resolved into her arresting apparition,
complete with the illusion of space and depth.

Lee stood before a mirror, hands clasped
behind her back, willing herself
to be her father's partner, to conceive
of herself as an aesthetic subject
and an object of scrutiny for the man
in whose eyes she saw herself mirrored.
She learned how to distance herself
from the use of her body
to which her love of him bound her.

Her art was born of her ability
to be subject and object at once.
She learned to picture herself as others saw her
and project herself as they wished to see her.
Her theatrical training in lighting,
costume, and stage design
added to her love of dance
and feeling for gesture, her memory
for the compositions of great paintings,
sensitivity to light and shadow,
the accidental and the ephemeral
enriched her work as model and photographer.

A mythology developed about her:
Condé Nast himself had plucked her
from the path of an oncoming car
and put her on the cover of *Vogue*.
For those who didn't know any better,
a lucky star seemed to shine over her.

Her childhood trauma burrowed deep
within her psyche. She no longer connected
the long-ago rape to her explosions of fury.
In the attack she'd gone numb,
as though she were observing herself
from outside her body, or it was a dream
from which she'd shortly awaken.
Her father told her that sex and love
were separate, and she believed him.
If she was sure of anything,
it was her father's love.

Her parents were unhappy. Theodore
was unfaithful. Florence gave her heart
to another man and tried to kill herself.
Theodore found her and saved her life.
Returning home from the hospital,
Florence was so angry she threw a chair
at the bed, denting the wall.

One hot July day when she was a teenager,
Lee was rowing with a boy on Upton Lake
when he jumped off the side of the boat
and disappeared. After the lake was dragged,
his drowned body was found. His mother
blamed Lee for her son's death.

As Lee's ocean liner departed New York
for France two years later,
a Canadian airman in love with her
swooped his biplane low
over the deck of the ship,
serenading her with a shower
of red roses before flying off
to pick up his pupil
at Roosevelt Airfield. Minutes later,
his plane spun into the ground,
killing both men.

A step ahead of tragedy, Lee stayed on the move.
She took risks, challenged herself, and didn't give in.
When war broke out, she was living with Roland
at Hampstead, near London. In their flat
they sheltered people bombed out

by the blitz. They took in Valentine,
Roland's first wife, a refugee from France,
and gave her a home for the rest of her life.

One night they put up a military photographer,
Dave Scherman from Brooklyn.
On contract with *Vogue*, Lee confessed
she longed to cover more than wartime fashion.
Dave advised her to apply to the U.S. Army
for accreditation as war correspondent,
and she was approved.

For the next two years, Lee and Dave
shared assignments and facilities
all over England, Scotland, and Ireland.
She was ten years older, and they fell in love.
Dave lived with her openly in Hampstead.
Lee insisted she could never be owned.
Roland accepted their arrangement
and took lovers of his own.

Roland's pacifist principles conflicted
with his sense of duty. His brother Beacus,
a seaman, saw action in Anzio
and was promoted to naval commander,
but Roland remained a noncombatant,
issuing reports to the military
about the use of camouflage in Italy.
Lee went to France with the Normandy invasion.
Her next assignment was St. Malô,
where she had a scoop, and the Germans were routed.
Dave joined her, landing from a U.S. warship.

Proud to serve her country.
Lee was as tough as the toughest soldier
in the male theater of war.
Dave and Lee arrived in Paris
the day it was liberated
and holed up at the Hotel Scribe
in adjoining rooms. She used hers
as a supply dump and slept in his.
The hotel had electricity, heat, and water
when the rest of Paris did not.
There she produced her dispatches for *Vogue*.

With her Rolleiflex around her neck,
Lee found photography second nature,
composing her images quickly,
calculating exposures from experience.
Writing was different. She raged at her drafts
and tore them up, despaired and drank to excess.
Her emotional scenes swept up everyone around her.
Dave described it like feeding his brain
through a meat grinder.
No one reading Lee's dispatches
would discern the chaos in which she'd created them.
She described soldiers ready for action,
grenades hanging on their lapels like Cartier clips,
menacing bunches of death.

Roland showed up to fetch Lee home,
but the war wasn't over,
and she was on a mission.
Lonely and jealous that her work
was more important than his,

Roland returned to England,
soon consumed by politics and infighting
among his artist friends.

The winter of 1944-45 was the worst of the war.
Lee was with the soldiers who liberated Dachau.
As she photographed the emaciated corpses
and living skeletons, she scanned the faces
to see if any of her friends were among them.
She recorded prisoners who died as she stood there.

At the edge of the camp, they found a train
that had left Auschwitz a month earlier
with more than two thousand prisoners.
On arrival in Dachau, the SS posted guards
with orders to shoot escapees. The GIs found
only one survivor. Lee snapped the photo
the medical examiner couldn't take,
too overcome with revulsion when the door
to the rail car was opened,
and the rotting corpses flopped out.

That night Dave and Lee found themselves
in Hitler's house in Berchtesgaden.
Dave took pictures of Lee bathing
in Hitler's bathtub, her boots stained
with the mud of Dachau soiling the bathmat.
It was the last time Dave and Lee worked together.

Lee followed the GIs into Austria,
while Dave returned to Paris, then London.
In Vienna after the war, Lee witnessed babies dying

for lack of medication. The persistent injustices,
the plight of homeless refugees inflamed her.
She wanted her work with Dave to continue.
First he refused, then reconsidered.
They proposed a joint project to Lee's editor,
but Roland, fearing he'd lose Lee forever,
persuaded Dave to kill the idea.

When Lee came home for a month,
tensions flared between her and Roland.
In her view, her work wasn't finished.
Roland felt envious and inadequate.
After a full-scale fight, with screaming
and slamming doors, Lee left for Paris.
Right away, Roland regretted their quarrel.
He wrote, begging her to return,
or just to write. He received no response.
Lee drafted letters, but never sent them.

Roland wrote again, this time to confess
he had fallen in love with another woman.
He asked if she was coming home.
She didn't reply. Dave cabled her,
Go Home. She cabled back, *OK.*

Lee returned from the war a broken woman.
She was sick, her skin a pasty white.
Her gums bled continually. Her hair fell out.
After a while her body got better,
but her spirit still suffered.
She took on new assignments
but had a hard time completing them.

The war might be over, but her war wasn't over.
She was surprised to find herself pregnant.
Though she'd had abortions in the past,
she hadn't thought it could happen to her
at nearly forty. She'd never wanted children,
even claimed to hate the sight of them,
but now she confessed to delight.

After she got pregnant, Lee and Roland called a truce.
When she returned to him to have his child,
she was still legally married to Aziz.
Aziz had accepted their separation years ago,
but refused to divorce her until another man
could take care of her. Poor Aziz! Because of Lee,
he'd impoverished himself. He'd made over
a portion of his business to her, sent her papers
to sign, but she'd never returned them,
and he'd had to relinquish his ownership.
Now he lived in modest circumstances,
but ever the gentleman, he didn't blame her.

He traveled to London from Cairo
to grant her a civil and religious divorce
to free her for marriage with Roland.
According to the Muslim ritual,
he circled the bed where she lay,
suffering from morning sickness.

Lee had faced perilous situations in war time
and peace time. By courage and quick wit,
she negotiated her way out of danger.
Held by the Russians, she matched them

drink for drink and won their respect.
Nothing, it seemed, could hold her back.

But she feared and loathed every aspect of maternity.
Throughout the pregnancy, she felt miserable.
She scheduled a caesarian section in advance
so she wouldn't have to give birth.
After Antony was born, she hired a nanny
so she wouldn't have to take care of him.
She never tried to nurse him.
She rarely showed him affection.
Sometimes it seemed to Antony
that she despised the sight of him.

Antony resented his distant father
and detested his cruel mother.
We hated each other with such attention
that it became an art form.
We lurked in ambush for each other,
never missing a chance to assassinate
each other's emotions in humiliating battles.

The war stole Lee's looks.
Beauty meant power and privilege,
seduction and attraction.
Her loveliness had always been
her calling card. She used it,
was used to it, and took it
for granted until it was gone,
when she minded the loss of it
more than she could admit.

The war hijacked Lee's love of fashion.
Before the war, she worked as a model
and fashion photographer.
She knew how to look good in clothes
and make clothes look desirable.
In the war, she found she liked wearing
a uniform and not thinking about it.
After the war, it was her rebellion not to care.
If her clothing was torn, stained,
or wrinkled, it didn't bother her.

Lee's interest in sex was next to go.
Once sex had meant freedom to her.
Like a man, she claimed sex as her right.
But after she became a mother, she lost interest.
She told Roland he was free to seek other partners.
She told him she didn't care. Or maybe
she got tired of being tied up.

Roland's grandfather, a painter, had lived on a farm.
As a boy, Roland thought it paradise
and dreamed of becoming a gentleman farmer.
After the war, he bought Farley Farm,
in Muddles Green, Sussex, south of London,
with a view over the chalk downs.
His week was spent in the London art world
with long weekends on the farm.
Lee preferred city life
and felt trapped on the farm.

The world was moving on, but Lee was stuck.
She took on assignments

but couldn't meet deadlines.
She created scenes and flew into tantrums.
She lost confidence in her abilities.
Roland decided it was time for her to stop.

Proud of publishing Lee's war dispatches,
Audrey, her *Vogue* editor, believed in her.
She was willing to accommodate her,
until Roland implored, *Please do not ask
Lee to write again. The suffering it causes her
and those around her is unbelievable.*

Audrey believed, *Lee was not meant to be married.
to have children, to live in the country.
She thought she wanted security,
but when she had it, she wasn't happy.*
But Lee had grown accustomed
to the support of wealthy men
and allowed Roland's interference
to put an end to the work
that was her source of achievement.

The war reminded Roland of his inadequacy.
He resented what it had done to Lee.
Lee lived in a welter of disorder.
Though terrified of mental illness
and suicidal, she refused psychiatric help
and numbed herself with drink.
Her anger went underground
and resurfaced as self-sabotage.

Since childhood, she had coped with trauma
by repression and separation.
Her courage in combat was unquestioned,
but confronted with her own psychology,
she was a coward. Roland's wish not to know
about her experiences compounded
her tendencies towards silence and secrecy.

The Surrealists had imagined they were living
on the edge, but they were only playing with fire.
The war took transgression to new levels.
It made men like William Seabrook, who liked
to play sadistic games with women, look silly.
The war destroyed Surrealism as a movement,
because games like that weren't amusing anymore.

After Lee ceased to have a *Vogue* contract,
she continued her work in art and photography
through her partnership with Roland.
Roland, dyslexic, struggled with reading and writing.
Lee organized exhibitions, charmed artists,
wrote copy, and took photographs for catalogs.
In matters of art, she and Roland saw eye-to-eye.

Picasso liked to lead friends on and reject them,
but he was in awe of Lee. In the thirties,
he'd been enough in love with her
to paint her portrait, and he couldn't get over
the fact the first American in uniform
he'd seen at the liberation of Paris was Lee.
Picasso gave Lee *carte blanche* to come to Mougins,
photograph him at work, and record

the clutter of objects that crowded his studio.
Because of Lee, Roland got permission
to produce Picasso's first biography.

Lee's culinary interests began in desert treks,
when she added spices to canned foods
to improve them. At Farley Farm, she amassed
a collection of 2,000 cookbooks and liked
to fall asleep curled up on the floor,
with a pile of them ranged around her.

On weekends, when they had company,
she'd start drinking before noon,
and after lunch, when Roland took guests
on long walks through the downs,
she'd be sleeping it off. She'd get up,
start drinking again, and dinner preparations
would last until late into the evening.
The guests would be cranky,
but all agreed when the food was served
that it was delicious and inventive.

Lee amused herself by inventing recipes
and entering competitions under pseudonyms.
Once she won all three prizes in a smorgasbord contest.
At dinner one evening, snobbish Cyril Connolly
complained about Americans who stuff themselves
with marshmallows and Coca Cola,
as he scooped up the last drops of ice cream
Lee served him. "It's delicious. What's in it?"
"Marshmallows and Coca Cola," Lee replied.

In later years, fending off queries
about her career, Lee claimed that decades
of her photos had been scrapped in office moves
by Condé Nast or otherwise lost in New York,
thrown out by the Germans in Paris,
or bombed and buried in the London blitz.

All the while 60,000 photos and negatives
and 20,000 items of memorabilia
were sitting in cardboard boxes
in the attic of her Sussex farmhouse.
Some believe she undervalued her work.
But she didn't destroy it; she deflected interest.
She had too many memories, too many regrets.
The past had become too great a burden.
She didn't care about posterity or her legacy.
Let someone else take care of that.

Roland denied that Lee's accomplishments
were equal to her male contemporaries.
"*We were the artists,*" he insisted. "*She was our muse.*"
Another reason to let the past stay buried.

In cooking, Lee found a physical world
as immersed in the body as sex,
as ephemeral and pleasurable.
Cooking took the place of sex for her,
another reason why she loved it so.

Music brought solace for wounds
that would never heal. Sometimes,
late at night, when she was drunk,

she would take a young woman
into her confidence, perhaps a daughter
of one of her friends, and break into sobs,
"*I got in over my head. I never could*
get the stench of Dachau out of my nostrils."

She yearned for a daughter
and made peace with her son
only after he returned to England
with a wife from New Zealand
after two years of traveling the world.
When Suzanne gave birth to a daughter,
Lee changed her mind about motherhood.
"*Towards the end of her life,* said her son,
thanks to my wife, we became friends.
But I didn't know her."

It wasn't until after Lee's death
that her son and daughter-in-law
discovered what was in the dusty boxes
in the attic at Farley Farm.
Children grow up in a different world
from their parents, and maybe it's not fair
to blame them for their lack of comprehension.
Parents don't understand their children either.
Antony couldn't forgive his mother's hatred.

"*The one that really haunts me*
is of an 18-year-old German soldier.
He died horribly, both his hands are blown up,
and on the back she has written,
'This is a good German, he's dead.'

I was shocked to the core that my mother
could write that about an 18-year-old boy."

Lee's hatred of the Nazis was intense,
but it was not as great as her self-loathing.
The balance is not equal.
The evidence speaks for itself.
We are more than our worst moments
and less than our best.

FRIDA

*"Love the earth and sun and the animals...
And your very flesh shall be a great poem."*
—Walt Whitman, *Preface to Leaves of Grass*

The address the woman at the market gave her
led to a stone house with a wooden door
on a rubbish-strewn street in Mexico City.

At the end of a long, dim hallway,
Frida came to a sunlit patio
alive with plants and birds
where she found her sister Maty
washing herself with a hose.

She'd not seen Maty since the day
she'd eloped at the age of fifteen.
Frida was seven when she helped her sister
escape through a balcony window
and fifteen when she found her again.
Their parents wouldn't forgive Maty
for fleeing their unhappiness.

Their father proposed to their mother
the night his first wife died in childbirth.
Three months later, when they married,
Matilde sent his infant daughter and her older sister
to be raised in a convent.

Guillermo wanted sons, but their only son died.
He had four more daughters with Matilde.
After each birth, Matilde escaped into illness.

The two older daughters raised their younger sisters.
Next-to-youngest Frida was her father's favorite,
dressed as a boy in family portraits
next to her more conventional sisters.

Frida was the only one
educated at the Preparatoria
among the elite like a favored son.
She commuted from Coyoacán
into the heart of Mexico City,
one of 35 girls among 2,000 boys.

After the Mexican Revolution,
the family began its slide into poverty,
when Guillermo lost his commission
documenting his adopted country's
architectural heritage. His beloved
Blue House had to be mortgaged.
Misanthropic, epileptic,
he retreated into failure,
while his shrewd, illiterate wife
managed the finances.

Frida was saucy, impertinent, lively,
despite her withered leg and limp
from polio. She was eighteen years old
and in love with an older student, Alejandro,
when one September afternoon, after school,
the rickety, wooden bus they were riding
was rammed by a street trolley.

They had been on another bus
when she missed her pink parasol,
and they got off to look for it.
After a while they gave up
and caught the next bus.
It was a long bus with benches
on either side. Struck in the middle,
the bus bent until it burst into pieces,
while the train kept moving.

It is a lie that one is aware of the crash,
a lie that one cries. In me there were no tears.
The crash bounced us forward, and a handrail
pierced me the way a sword pierces a bull.
A man saw me having a tremendous hemorrhage.
He carried me and put me on a billiard table
until the Red Cross came for me.

The train's steel handrail broke off,
entering Frida's abdomen
and exiting her vagina.
Her pelvis and spinal column
were broken in three places,
and her collarbone was fractured.
Her third and fourth ribs were broken.
Her right leg had eleven fractures.
Her right foot was dislocated and crushed.

The impact of the crash stripped
the clothes from her body.
A packet of gold leaf
carried by a painter spilled open,

sprinkling her naked, bleeding body
with flecks of gold. Seeing her,
people cried, *La bailarina!*
Alejandro covered her with his coat.
Few thought she would survive.

When they heard the news,
her parents fell ill. Her mother
didn't speak for a month. Her father
took to his bed for twenty days.
Sister Adriana fainted.
Only Maty came to see her
and returned every day.

The hospital was once a convent,
dark and bare. In a gloomy ward,
Frida lay flat on her back in a plaster cast,
in a box like a coffin. During the day,
Maty nursed her and made her laugh,
but at night death danced around her bed.

Guillermo and Matilde
were consumed with Frida's medical costs.
Had she been a rich man's daughter,
the doctors would have been more careful.
After what was deemed a miraculous recovery,
she was sent home without exam or Xray.
A year later it was discovered
three vertebrae were misaligned.

In the Kahlo family,
Guillermo and Matilde claimed all

the psychic space for suffering.
Discharged from the hospital
after a month, Frida felt trapped at home
with her unhappy parents, far away
from her friends, confined to bed,
lonely, isolated, and in pain.

A little while ago, I was a child
who went about in a world of colors.
Everything was mysterious
and something was hidden,
guessing what it was
was a game for me.
How terrible it is to know suddenly
as if a bolt of lightning
elucidated the earth.
Everything is bland and lucid.
My friends grew up slowly,
but I became old in an instant.
I live on a painful planet,
translucent as ice.

For the rest of her life, Frida suffered
from pain and fatigue.
She wore plaster casts, heavy braces,
and corsets of leather and metal
to support her spine.
The sole of her right shoe
had to be built up an inch higher
than the left so she could walk.
She cut holes in the shoe
to ease the sores on her foot.

Despite 22 surgeries
to repair damage from the accident
and the doctors' incompetence,
her health deteriorated,
until her death 29 years later.

Of the betrayals after the accident,
the worst was Alejandro.
To him as to no one else,
she poured out her heart.
But he was unequal to her need.
He fled to study in Europe
without telling her goodbye.

In the corner of his studio,
Guillermo kept a box of oil paints,
a palette, and some brushes in a vase.
Ever since she was a child,
Frida had cast her eye on his art supplies.
She persuaded him to let her use them.
Her mother hired a carpenter to make
an easel that attached to her bed
so she could paint lying down.

Frida was gifted with talents and aptitudes.
The accident ended her possibilities.
Painting became her child of necessity.
She painted small because small
was what she could manage.
She preferred to work in private.
With painting she could tell her truth
without having to speak.

Once, when she was a child
confined to her room with polio,
Frida breathed on the window glass
and in the vapor, she drew a door.
In her mind she went through the door
and across the street. She stood in front
of the dairy with the sign, "Pinzon"
and entered the letter "O."
Suddenly she found herself
in the interior of the earth.

A little girl was waiting for her.
Smiling, the girl listened as Frida
confided her secret problems.
The girl danced without music,
and Frida followed her.
When it was time to leave,
Frida returned the way she had come.
Back in her room, she blurred the glass
with her hand, and the door disappeared.
The illusion was gone, but the feeling
of friendship persisted.

Convalescent after the accident,
Frida remembered the dear companion
who accompanied her to the depths,
in whom she could confide
without being abandoned.

All aspects of her life
Frida transformed into art.
In her proliferating images,

the designs of her house and garden,
her clothes and her hair, her adornments
and her animal companions,
she created visions of enchantment.

After Alejandro left her,
she fell in love with an artist
so big she could hide behind him,
old enough to be her father,
and prosperous enough to support her
and help her family.
Of unquestioned stature himself,
Diego Rivera saw greatness in Frida:
*The monumental is expressed
in the smallest dimensions.*

In the first days of their love,
the electricity of their kisses
turned on and off the streetlamps
during their evening strolls
through Coyoacán's avenues.

When Diego asked for permission
to marry Frida, her father replied,
*"My daughter is sick, and all her life
she will be sick. She is intelligent,
but not pretty. Think it over,
and if you wish to marry her,
I give you my permission."*
Alone of her family,
Guillermo attended the wedding.
Frida wore a skirt and blouse

and *rebozo* borrowed from a maid,
draped to conceal her apparatus.

Her braided hair and floral headpieces,
dangling earrings and heavy necklaces,
square-cut blouses with ribbons
and ornaments, and long skirts
were how Tehuana women dressed.
It was Frida's family's custom to wear
these clothes on special occasions.
Frida's costume became her emblem,
an expression of family ties
and national loyalty. In the gray streets
of New York and Paris, Detroit
and San Francisco, she attracted attention
like a tropical bird out of its element.
Sometimes she sewed bells to her petticoats
that made a tinkling music as she walked.

Frida liked to spend hours getting ready
to go out. Pleasure was in the preparation,
as essential as the performance.
Her attire gave her the appearance of gaiety.
Children followed her through city streets,
expecting to be led to a circus.

But appearances can be deceiving.
Her clothing concealed the broken parts
of her body and the braces and corset
she wore for support. The more
she was suffering or worse she was feeling,
the more adornment she would wear.

At the end of her life,
when she could no longer leave her bed,
she still dressed like a doll for visitors.

Frida met Diego when she was a student
and he got his first big commission,
a mural for her school's auditorium.
Defying Lupe, his watchful wife,
she sneaked in to watch him at work.
When they met again eight years later,
he remembered the bold schoolgirl.
Then she had been mischievous,
but now she was serious. Showing him
three portraits, she demanded his criticism:
I'm neither an art lover nor an amateur,
but a girl who must work for her living.

I had to restrain myself from praising
her as much as I wanted.
It was obvious she was an authentic artist.
A week later, I went to see her.
Her room, her paintings, her presence
filled me with wonderful joy.
I did not know it then,
but Frida had already become
the most important person in my life.

Diego put art at the service of politics.
In monumental murals he celebrated
workers and peasants, his native Mexico.
Yet he preferred to live in New York.
Although he was a Communist,

his most important patrons
were American capitalists.
His productivity was astonishing,
his appetites legendary.
Women were attracted to him
in spite of his ugliness.
He was unfaithful,
and Frida was jealous,
though she made friends
of most of her rivals.

Diego's commissions brought them
to San Francisco, New York, and Detroit.
In every city, they were feted
by wealthy supporters of art and culture.
In 1932, the Museum of Modern Art
gave Diego a blockbuster retrospective.
Diego was in his element, but Frida was not.
The darkness of American cities
depressed her. Walking was difficult,
and she couldn't bear the heat and cold.
She longed for children, but her body
was too damaged to bear a child.
Her pregnancies ended in miscarriage
or therapeutic abortions.

In the excruciating heat of a New York
summer, she sat in the bathtub
soaking her feet, in agonizing pain,
while Diego kept trysts with Louise Nevelson.
The public flocked to watch Diego at work
on a mural commissioned by Nelson Rockefeller

to celebrate "Men at the Crossroads
looking with Hope and High Vision
to the Choosing of a New and Better Future."
Diego portrayed that future as a Marxist utopia
and the US as evil and corrupt.

When Diego's design was publicized,
the sturdy scaffolding in the RCA building
was replaced by a flimsier structure.
Diego shielded his mural from the public,
transforming his sketch of a labor leader
into a portrait of Lenin. When Nelson objected,
Diego refused to remove the likeness.
Nelson paid the artist's fee and fired him,
and the mural was destroyed.
Diego was astounded. He never dreamed
Nelson would call his bluff. He vowed
to use his fee to paint another mural
and threw himself into activism,
while the Communists attacked him
for accepting commissions from millionaires.

At Frida's insistence, they returned to Mexico
over Diego's objections. He punished
Frida by seducing her younger sister.
Cristina's husband had left her,
and she was living with her children
and widowed father in the Blue House
in Coyoacán Diego had bought for them.

The more I loved a woman,
the more I wanted to hurt her.

Frida was the most obvious victim
of this disgusting trait.

In time Frida forgave her sister
because she needed her.
Eventually she divorced Diego,
and a year later remarried him.
Drama and farce defined their marriage.
On their honeymoon, painting a mural
in Cuernavaca, Diego seduced his assistant,
but when Frida slept with Noguchi,
Diego brandished a pistol,
threatening to shoot the sculptor.

Even more than passion or love,
art bound Frida and Diego together.
It was a hard time to be a woman
in the art world. Diego guided Frida
and steadied her. He believed
in her greatness more than in his own.
For the catalog of her first exhibition,
he wrote: *I recommend her to you,*
not as a husband, but as an enthusiastic
admirer of her work, acid and tender,
hard as steel and delicate and fine
as a butterfly's wing, and profound
and cruel as the bitterness of life.

After her unresolved injuries
and ongoing surgeries,
sex required imagination,
and men weren't always willing

to put her pleasure first.
The only man who came close
to supplanting Diego in Frida's heart
was Nikolas Muray. An immigrant
photographer like her father
and Olympic fencing champion,
Nick was on his third divorce
when they met in Mexico and fell in love.
Nick excelled at portraits, and he made
magnificent photographs of her
in Mexico and later in New York.

Like a peacock spreading its train,
Frida radiated an outward joy
that concealed an inward sadness,
even indifference. But with Nick,
Frida allowed herself to be fully seen.
She could confide her deepest secrets—
her misery and anguish with Diego,
her ceaseless pain and endless fears.
She trusted Nick, but he let her down
like the others. Diego was his excuse:
Of the three of us, there was only two of you.
Your tears told me that when you heard his voice.
The one of me is eternally grateful for the Happiness
that half of you so generously gave.

Some guests repaid the Riveras' hospitality
with bad behavior. Leon Trotsky
was a dirty old man with wandering hands.
Frida looked on him as a father figure,
but he abused her and shamed his wife.

André Breton, the dean of surrealism,
was a freeloader and a thief, who stole
art off the walls of Mexican churches
and smuggled Aztec artifacts to Paris
which he sold at a profit. Frida
referred to him as a "cockroach,"
but she loved his beautiful wife
Jacqueline, who had to divorce André
to realize herself as an artist.

Encouraged by Diego, Frida traveled
to Paris on her own for the show
André had promised her, only to find
he'd made no plans and hadn't paid the fee
to get her paintings out of customs.
In Mexico City, the Bretons were allowed
a whole wing of the Riveras' house.
Frida expected a similar reception.
At first she thought the Bretons' apartment
was André's studio. There was no place to live,
to place for Jacqueline to work. Forced
to share their daughter's tiny bedroom,
Frida fled to a hotel, but the bathroom
was down the hall, and she came down
with a kidney infection. She was rescued
by Marcel Duchamp and Mary Reynolds
and welcomed into Mary's beautiful home
near the catacombs, with a private garden
and wood-burning fireplace that reminded
her of her Blue House in Mexico.

Although Frida never painted
the public scene of her crucifixion,
it is the ghostly negative behind
the portraits of her wounded body,
bleeding, suffering, and exposed.
Even when her face is streaked by tears,
her gaze remains inward and unknowable,
while her body is screaming.

For the rest of her life,
she preserved the dead fetuses
of her aborted children in jars
of formalin in her wardrobe.
My painting carries the message of pain.
I will sell everything for nothing.
Nothing has a name.
I lost three children.
Paintings substituted for all this.
Children are the days
and here is where I end.

From you to my hands
I go over all your body,
and my blood is the miracle
that travels in the veins of the air
from my heart to yours.

BEING RUTH ASAWA

*"We do not always create 'works of art,' but rather experiments;
it is not our ambition to fill museums: we are gathering experience."*
— Josef Albers

*"When I'm working on a problem, I never think about Beauty,
I think only how to solve the problem. But when I have finished,
if the solution is not beautiful, I know it is wrong."*
— R. Buckminster Fuller

I remember sitting in the back
of my father's horse-drawn leveler,
dragging my big toe in the dirt path
between fields, making looping,
hourglass designs. This was in the 1930s,
outside Los Angeles, California.

My father leased land he couldn't own
because of the law against foreigners.
My mother was a Japanese picture bride,
betrothed on the promise of a photograph.
I was fourth of their seven children.

Our father built our house of board-and-batten,
with a paper ceiling and a tin roof.
He knew how to use water wisely
and grew beautiful vegetables from that earth.

We toiled alongside our parents,
planting, weeding, harvesting,
nurturing the soil.
But our father was cheated at market.
We were so poor we salvaged

nails from shipping crates.
We trapped gophers for meat.

Through persistence and perseverance,
our father increased his leasehold
to eighty acres. He hired laborers.
We owned two cars and two tractors.
He was a father to his brother's five children
as well as to us, after his brother died.

After Pearl Harbor was bombed,
he made a big hole in the ground
where he buried our Kendo swords and gear.
He burned the beautiful Japanese books
on the tea ceremony and flower design
and the precious dolls and badminton paddles
my sister had brought from Japan
just months before.

One Sunday in February 1942,
two men in dark suits surprised us
as we worked in the fields.
They took our father by the arm
and marched him to the house.
They watched him eat lunch.
He finished his meal with a slice
of my sister's lemon meringue pie,
and then they drove him away.

I learned later they were FBI
and suspected our father
of being a traitor.

He disappeared from our lives.
Four years passed before
we saw him again.

Soon, with thousands of others,
we were assigned to a detention camp
in Santa Anita. We lost almost everything
we owned. We lived in the stables
of a converted racetrack
surrounded by barbed wire.
Hair from the horses' manes and tails
stuck between cracks in the walls.
In the summer heat, the smell
of horses was overpowering.

The excuse for separating us
from our homes and livelihoods
was that the U.S. was at war with Japan
where our parents were from.
Yet there was no similar removal
of Italian or German Americans.

In the camp, I noticed three men
who liked to sit together high
in the grandstand of the racetrack,
balancing sketchpads on their knees,
drawing pictures with pieces of charcoal.
They didn't seem to mind the dust
that blew up from the track, or the sun,
or if I sat with them. They encouraged me.
That was how I learned I was an artist, too.

They were my teachers—
Tom Okamoto, Chris Ishii, James Tanaka—
Disney artists who'd drawn *Pinocchio,*
Fantasia, Dumbo, Donald Duck,
and *Mickey Mouse*—now suspected
of being "enemies of the people."

Yet I saw how when they worked,
worry fled. In the midst of hardship,
their concentration made a peaceful space
where something unexpected
and beautiful might happen.

Wire selected me,
not the other way around.
We had it on the farm,
and even as a child
I noticed how useful it is
and how transparent a barrier.

Wire starts out as a line,
a boundary between two places,
inside and outside, left and right,
But wire can also be transformed
into a three-dimensional object.

In the summer of 1947,
when I was an art student
at Black Mountain College,
I joined a public service project
to teach art to children in Toluca, Mexico.
In the market I noticed the wire baskets

made by farmers to carry eggs and produce.
They needed no tools but their own hands.

They taught me how to wrap wire
in even loops around a dowel.
Interlocking loops formed rows
which could be varied by size and shape
by adding loops or subtracting them.
It was like crocheting without a hook
or knitting without needles.

When I returned to Black Mountain,
my first sculptures were baskets
like the ones the Mexican farmers made.
When I joined the beginning to the end,
they became rounded, like fruits.
Next they stood up and took flight.
They asked me to consider,
what is inside, and what is outside?
I have spent my life finding out,
layering form within form,
voluptuous, swelling.
Was I thinking of motherhood,
of my own children? Yes, and no.
Making art is a different mental process.
Any artist will understand.

My great teacher, Josef Albers,
taught the use of negative space,
beauty in repetition, and the cultivation
of a deep awareness.
He wasn't interested in feelings.

If you want to express yourself,
do it on your own time, he said,
not in my class.

Some of the students resented this,
but I come from a culture
where personal feelings are hidden.

Albers said, *Draw what you see,*
not what you know.
Even black will change.
Never see anything in isolation.
Define an object by defining
the space around it.

I understood this, too.
As a child, I studied calligraphy
where we learned to consider the spaces
between the brushstrokes
as well as the brushstrokes themselves.

Albers also said, *Art doesn't know*
progress or graduation. Year after year
he taught the same courses—
design, color, drawing and painting,
presenting us with the same problems,
concepts, and assignments,
but each time was never the same.

I learned that nothing is ever settled
in life or in art. Sometimes adversity
yields an advantage. It's like looking

for a light in darkness.
Your eyes will sometimes betray you,
but eventually you'll find a way out.
Our detention in Santa Anita was temporary.
After five months, we were sent
to the Rohwer Relocation Center
in the swampland of southeast Arkansas,
where eight thousand Japanese immigrants
and Americans of Japanese descent
lived in communal barracks.

We shared lavatories, a laundry,
a kitchen, and dining hall.
The soil between the barracks
turned to black muck when it rained.
Cypress trees grow in the bayous,
and creeks snaked through fields
worked by sharecroppers.

The eerie beauty of that landscape,
half earth and half water,
has stayed with me,
the gnarled cypress knees
that grew straight up
from their hidden roots
through dark water.

We searched the swamps
for the most unusual shapes.
Sanded and hand-polished,
they became doorstops,
useful and ornamental.

My mother had brought seeds,
and we planted a garden.
We kept chickens and a pig.
At Rohwer, we went to school.
Every morning we pledged allegiance
to the flag of the United States of America.
When we came to the end,
"with liberty and justice for all,"
we added under our breath,
"except for us."

Living with my family on the farm,
I had been an obedient Japanese girl.
At Rohwer, I learned to question authority.
Imprisoned as un-American,
I became American. Living the way
we did, without our father,
our family ties loosened.
Students at Rohwer were allowed
to attend college, if the college
was in the middle of the country.
The Quakers provided assistance.
In 1943, my sister Lois left for Iowa.
Chiyo followed her. I was next.

I picked the Milwaukee State Teachers College,
because it was the cheapest
in the catalog. I boarded with a family
as a live-in maid. Three years passed—
my father was released, the war ended,
but I was told I couldn't graduate.
Because of my Japanese background,
no one would hire me as a teacher.

Before I left Rohwer for college,
our teacher, Mrs. Beasley, told us
not to harbor any bitterness
from what had been done to us.
It was wrong, but to dwell on it
would only hurt us and hold us back.

All I had strived for was destroyed
when I wasn't allowed to graduate.
But what seemed the collapse
of my hopes was the prelude
to my transformation.
There were two doors,
and I opened both. They seemed
to lead down separate paths
but, in fact, they intersected.

In the summer of 1945,
my Milwaukee friends Elaine and Ray
wanted me to come with them
to Black Mountain College
in North Carolina,
but I went to Mexico City
with my sister Lois instead.
I studied design with Clara Porset,
a Cuban artist at the University of Mexico.
Clara had also been to Black Mountain.
The next summer, I went there, too.

Some educational experiments
are destined to flower and fade.
Black Mountain College

had a brief lifespan.
I was one of the lucky ones.

College life was like detention camp
turned inside out. The college
was also land-rich and dirt poor.
We were encouraged to find ways
to do what we wanted
with the few resources we had.
Teachers and students ate together,
and everyone had to work.
I gave haircuts to students and teachers,
worked in the school laundry,
and woke in the early morning
to churn butter and make cheese.
How the Europeans loved soft butter
and buttermilk at breakfast!

Many of the teachers were refugees.
Their culture made the college what it was.
Without the war, it would not have happened.
For a brief time, while it existed,
it was a haven for those who had suffered
because of their race, religion, or skin color.

My parents' Buddhism consisted
of rituals they never explained.
At Black Mountain College,
we learned the precepts of Buddhism.
My studies gave me insight
into the religion of my ancestors.
There was harmony and affinity

between the principles of my college
and the values of my heritage.

Rising before dawn
to make butter for breakfast,
I would knock on Albers' door
to wake him on my way to the barn
so he could photograph the fog
lying low over the mountains.
He would snap a few pictures
and go back to sleep.

When the cold fog
from San Francisco Bay
comes rolling in
through the big windows
of the high-ceilinged living room
of our brown shingled house
on Castro Street, I sometimes
remember the early morning
mountain fog in North Carolina.

At Black Mountain College,
I explored the land around me
as I had not done since childhood,
observing the trees and bushes,
vines and wildflowers. One day,
after I'd been there a year,
I was walking on a forest path
when I felt someone's eyes on me.
I turned and found myself
looking directly into his gaze.

It was Albert Lanier.
He had been watching me
before I noticed him.

Our backgrounds and upbringing
couldn't have been more different,
yet we never had any doubts
about our love for each other.
We knew what we would be facing
as an interracial couple raising a family,
but Albert was an architect and builder
and used to finding a way,
and I knew how to work hard.
We weren't likely to give up.

On a rainy summer day in 1948,
Albert and I watched from a ridge
with the rest of the college,
while our teacher, Buckminster Fuller,
connected the designated points
of a dome he had designed
out of strips of Venetian blinds.
When it failed to rise, he didn't give up.
The next summer he returned
with different solutions,
and this time, the dome stayed up.
There is no success without failure;
you succeed when you stop failing.

At Black Mountain College,
Albert built a Minimum House
with cheap industrial materials

and what was at hand. He diverted
a creek to flow around the house.

The house took a year to complete.
There was a large room for living
and sleeping, a kitchen, a bath,
and closets. Albert constructed a terrace
of flat fieldstone and two walls
of brown fieldstone striped with lichen
that he collected in the woods.
I advised him how to place the stones
to make a pattern, side by side
and up and down.

When Minimum House was finished,
Albert left to learn the building trades
in San Francisco, where it was legal
for us to marry. I planned to join him
in a year. Bucky Fuller designed
our wedding ring as his gift to us—
a black Lake Huron stone in a setting
formed by three "As" for "Asawa."

I felt I needed to warn Albert
what it meant to marry me:
My parents dare to be tolerant
because we have all suffered intolerance.
I no longer want to nurse such wounds.
I now want to wrap fingers
cut by aluminum shavings,
and hands scratched by wire.
Only these things produce tolerable pains.

You will have to look at me
on the streetcar or bus when you
hear someone shout, 'dirty Jap.'
I hope we never have to experience it,
but expect it, do not fear it.

I've overcome most of the fear.
This attitude has made me
a citizen of the universe,
by which I grow infinitely smaller
than if I belonged to a family,
province, or race. I can allow myself
not to be hurt by ugly remarks,
because I no longer identify
as a Japanese or American.

Our wedding took place two days
after my arrival, on July 3, 1949,
in a loft over the onion warehouse
that would be our first home.
I knew I wanted a large family.
Josef and Anni Albers,
who were childless by choice,
were skeptical. Before Albert left
Black Mountain, Albers took him aside
and said, *"Don't ever let Ruth stop working."*

Albert's work made mine possible.
We had six children in nine years:
Xavier, Aiko, Hudson, Adam,
Addie, and Paul. Raising children,
growing a garden, and making art

were all connected for me.
I created my sculptures
with my children around me.
I wanted them to understand
that art does not have to be
separate from the rest of life.
It can be as ordinary
and essential as breathing.

Bucky worked by trial and error,
Albers was interested in ideas
that didn't have a shape yet.
My ideas come from nature.
I start with general principles
that apply to anything I do.
Instead of forcing a design
onto my material,
I try to become background,
like a supportive parent
who enables the child to express itself.

Each material has a quality of its own.
By combining it or putting it next
to another material, I change it
or give it another personality,
without destroying either one.
When I separate them again,
they return to what they are.
It's the same with people.
You don't change someone's personality,
but combined with other people,
a person will take on different features.

The intent is not to alter,
but to bring out another aspect.

A line can enclose space,
while letting air remain air.
My wire sculptures
are a continuous surface.
I begin from the inside,
and as it takes shape,
it comes out and in again
while remaining, essentially, itself.
What interests me
are the proportions.

I folded origami as a child,
but my folded sculptures
come from my work with Albers.
We folded paper in the European way,
which is structural.
We learned about the strength
of certain angles.
You can fold a sheet of paper
so you can stand on it,
as if it were made of wood.
With paper, you can easily change
the folded angle, but metal is rigid.
You fold metal just once.

My friends Paul and Virginia
brought a desiccated plant
from Death Valley for me to draw.
The gnarled trunk branched off

symmetrically, ending in feathery fronds.
To understand its structure,
I modeled it in wire, which led
to my tied metal sculptures.

I start with as many as a thousand
strands of wire in a single bundle.
Using a pair of pliers
to cut and twist the wires,
I divide the bundle into thirds.
I continue to divide each branch
until only two strands are left.
I tie each joint with the same wire.
No solder is used.
When I create the tied center,
I have already made a decision.

It interests me to work out
variations of the same idea,
instead of following different ideas.
My sculptures are meant to be
suspended from the ceiling,
mounted on a wall, or on a base.
Bronze wire stays green a long time.
Brass wire turns dark. Immersing it
in an electrically charged sulfuric bath
leaves a greenish cast. The ends,
dipped in resin, resemble raindrops.
I asked the plating company
to run the electric current backwards,
creating a rough surface.

One quiet Sunday morning,
scavenging for materials
on a San Francisco street,
I found coils of enameled copper wire
on a sidewalk outside a bar.
They came from the insides
of smashed-up slot machines
that the city had recently outlawed
and ranged in color from rust-red
to purple and blue-back.

To be alert to my surroundings
is to be aware of opportunity.
When I was a child on the farm,
I shaped wire into rings and bracelets.
At Black Mountain we were encouraged
to use what we could find and was at hand.
When I worked in the college laundry,
I made drawings using the BMC stamp.
Albers' concept of the meander
influenced my studies of sequences,
patterns and contrasts, curves and reversals,
and optical illusions that "swindle the eye."

As the last rays of sunlight
cast shadows across my living room,
I sit cross-legged on the floor,
with the wire in my lap
and my hands on the wire,
my children around me,
reading or doing their homework,
playing or practicing the piano.

Above us, my wire sculptures tremble
and sway, in a dance with the air.
I feel they are protecting us,
like household gods.

I am often asked how I can bear
the tedium of my artistic process.
Farm work is by nature
tedious and repetitive,
and I grew up on a farm,
planting a thousand seeds at a time,
pulling hundreds of weeds,
harvesting fruit and vegetables
by the bushel. As I work,
I fall into a rhythm,
and the tedium becomes absorbing.

At Rohwer, I was proud of how well
I strung my beans on the trellis I made,
working from the bottom to the middle
to the top. I often construct
my sculptures in the same way.

My process is about the cultivation
of patience and stillness,
of learning to be nonreactive
and sit with discomfort,
and it has made me a better wife,
daughter, mother, teacher, and friend.

I tell women who want to make art,
Don't wait until it's too late,

and you don't have the energy.
You don't need long stretches of time.
Learn how to use your small snatches of time
as they are given to you, and they will add up.

After the war, my parents never got back
the leases they lost. They started over
working for someone else in Arizona.
They were simple people.
They wanted me to be lucky,
not in money or honors, but in life.

When I work, I am at one
with the spirit of my material.
Don't be afraid of the unknown.
The unknown is what will free you.

RUTH AND IMOGEN

RUTH:

When I married Albert Lanier
and we moved to San Francisco,
it was as if we leapt
into an entirely new existence
that was nothing like our families.

All my life, I've been blessed
with mentors—my teachers
in the public schools in Norwalk,
the Disney cartoonists at Santa Anita,
my teachers at Rohwer and in Milwaukee
and Black Mountain College.

It was the same in San Francisco.
Just when I needed her
and I didn't know it,
Imogen showed up.

We met through her son, Rondal,
a photographer hired by Albert's firm.
By then we'd been in San Francisco
for over a year. Albert's hopes of working
for himself hadn't panned out, and I'd given
birth to our twins, Xavier and Aiko.

When Albert praised Rondal's work,
Rondal replied, "You must meet my mother."
One afternoon soon after that, the doorbell rang.

I answered it with a baby on each arm.
A woman with wispy white hair
stood framed by the doorway,
bearing a jar of Satsuma plum jam
made from the fruit of her own tree.

She wore a cotton print dress
and a cable-knit sweater.
Her black lace-up shoes were sprinkled
with white construction dust
from work in the street.
Before she entered my house,
she wiped her shoes with a handkerchief.
That was how I met Imogen Cunningham.
A Rolleiflex hung from a leather strap
around her neck, its two vertical lenses
like Cyclops' eyes. That day
she did not take pictures,
but a few months later I wrote to Celia,
my friend in Milwaukee:

A photographer came to photograph
a piece of wire sculpture
and took pictures of the babies.
We saw the proofs last week,
and they are very good.
She has a brief and biting tongue
and all of her senses are alertly attuned
to react instantaneously.

Although I was 24 and she was 67,
Imogen and I became instant friends.

She championed me when art critics
labeled me a housewife, and my sculptures
were dismissed as crafts.

She said my history drew her to me.
One of her closest friends
was a Japanese artist and architect
who'd also been interned at Santa Anita.
She had kept his belongings safe
for him until after the war.

Imogen had three sons, including twins.
That was another bond between us.
For years she'd struggled to be artist,
wife, and mother. Her husband, Roi Partridge,
couldn't bear her success. After they married,
she closed her Seattle studio.

In San Francisco, she made delicate close-ups
of flora and fauna in her backyard garden.
They were exhibited and celebrated,
and her career was relaunched.
While she was in New York
on assignment for *Vanity Fair*,
Roi filed for divorce in Reno.

Imogen was soured on men and marriage.
When she learned I was using
my married name to exhibit my work,
she was appalled. Albert agreed.
It made no sense, he said, to have
a French name and an Asian face.

Eventually Albert won Imogen over.
We made an agreement—
for the next three years
she would photograph my work.
In return Albert would make
renovations to her house.

Imogen's example helped me
find my way as an artist and a mother.
She showed me how to transform
frugality into meaningful elegance.
She taught me that poverty
is a state of mind, and you are poor
only if you dwell on it.
Her artistic spirit pervaded
every aspect of her existence,
enlivening her sons' upbringing
and enriching their environment.

We had much in common—
dance, children, and gardens.
Introducing me to his mother,
Albert had said, "She'd rather dance
than eat." Imogen, too, had a love
of movement. As a photographer,
she used light to create life.
In some of her pictures, my sculptures
seem to grow and I to diminish.
They surround me, protect me, hide me.
The light strikes them, and I am in the shadows.
In others, I am at work, and they are in progress.
When I touch them, they come to life.

When I met Imogen, she was already old.
I used to amuse myself by imagining
what she was like when she was my age.
Appearances notwithstanding,
she was one of the most passionate
people I've ever known. I look
at her pictures of me and my work
and my children, and I see love,
concentration, pride, joy, astonishment,
and sensuality. It's as if I can see myself thinking.
How did she do it? I don't know.
But I do know that she was fearless
in the same way that I am.

IMOGEN:

To photograph some of Ruth's sculptures,
I used a reverse-negative process
to create a gelatin silver print,
in which they appear illuminated
against a black background.
Reversing the process again,
I printed a positive, where the dark sculptures
cast shadows against a light backdrop.

Growing up, I had a scientific bent.
At the University of Washington,
I majored in chemistry and made lantern slides
for the botany department, assembling
a visual catalog of its specimens
in the days before slide projectors.
A sheet of glass was sensitized

with a gelatin silver emulsion.
The plate was exposed to a negative,
resulting in a positive transparency
valued for its complexity and tonal range.
I appreciated the subtlety of the process
and continued my work in that medium
when I went out on my own.

I wrote Ruth's recommendation
for a Guggenheim fellowship:
She is an unfailingly creative person
and an indomitable worker.
Although young, she has maturity
and a balance that few achieve.
The more she undertakes,
the more she accomplishes.

I was certain she'd be selected,
but each time she applied,
she was passed over.
It's true I was hardly objective.
After twenty years of fruitless efforts,
I confessed to the committee:
I may be too involved in her work
to be a cool observer,
as I have photographed much of the sculpture,
making it mine as well as hers.

Success and failure
are matters of perspective,
and perspectives change.
When I met Ruth, I recognized

an old soul, despite her youth.
She credited my example,
but I think I learned more from her
than she from me. Her energy
and industry astonished me.
It came from her upbringing
as a farmer's daughter.
She seemed to draw strength
from the earth up through her body.
She brought life into everything she touched,
and everything she made had a wholeness
and satisfaction to it. I worried
that her wish to have a large family
and be an artist wouldn't come true,
but she thrived in the ferment of family life,
calming disorder and confusion,
radiant in her sense of concentration.

In the late 1950s, Ruth and Albert bought
a country property in Guerneville,
near the Russian River, in Sonoma County,
an area they'd come to know and love
through Marguerite Wildenhain,
a potter they'd befriended at Black Mountain,
who'd established a ceramics studio
at nearby Pond Farm. The Laniers' property
had an underground stream, a redwood grove,
a barn with aluminum siding where they lived,
and a shed where they kept their tools.
Some of my happiest times were my visits
to Guerneville. As old age advanced,
it meant more and more to me.

Their marriage was a true partnership,
something I never had. Albert was steadfast,
and he had a gift, like Ruth, of inspiring people
to do what they never thought themselves capable of.
When he was renovating their house on Castro Street,
Albert enlisted the help of his two older sons,
friends, schoolboys, a few union workers,
odd jobbers, and alcoholics who stashed empties
on the site that kept turning up for years.

He used recycled and repurposed materials
to transform the house from a two-bedroom
cottage with a loft for a pipe organ into a home
with light and space for a family of eight,
where Ruth's sculptures hung from the ceiling
of the loft, as in a cathedral of art
whose tall windows looked out to the bay,
and there was an attic bedroom for the girls
and a dormitory for the boys, suspended
between the workshop-studio and backyard
garden planted with rose, iris, wisteria,
bleeding heart, rosemary, and columbine
in one of the sunniest spots in San Francisco.

Their home encouraged a creative family life
to which all contributed. In the summers
Ruth and her children picked apples
in the orchards near Guerneville
to pay for their school clothes.
They labored in their garden,
growing fruits and vegetables.
Ruth believed in drawing every day.

"Whether or not you become an artist,
drawing will make you better at whatever
you choose to do," she told her children.

She and her children carved two oversized
redwood doors for the Castro Street house
in a wavelike pattern of moving spirals
that morph into shapes of a human face
to conceal the doorknobs. Ruth drew
the meandering design in white chalk,
and the children helped her to carve
and burnish it. Once an area was chiseled,
a small torch burned the rough edges smooth,
raising the grain and softening the contours,
and then it was cleaned with a wire brush.
Ruth allowed five-year-old Adam,
who was obsessed with bees, to poke
"bee holes" into the wood. Participation
was more important than perfection.

Over the years Albert bought adjacent properties,
removing the fences that divided their backyards,
creating a family compound and communal garden.
A nurturing energy seemed to radiate from their home,
expressed not only in their bountiful harvests
shared with grateful recipients like me,
but in their abiding concern for their community.

As a student in the Norwalk public schools,
Ruth took dance, music, and art classes
taught by working artists. By the time
her children started school in San Francisco,

that commitment to the arts was gone.
Ruth's activism focused on arts education.
She began a workshop in her children's school
that grew to a city-wide initiative and led
to the founding of a public arts high school.

The exuberant mermaids nursing their babies
in her Ghirardelli Square fountain
were scorned by the landscape architect.
He would have preferred a phallic tower
spraying water forty feet high.
For once the male vision didn't triumph.
When she designed the fountain
with its gentle mists and looping jets of water,
its sinuous plants and sea creatures,
and delicate webbed tails
of the mermaids and merbabies,
Ruth said she was thinking of children
and chocolates, and of the Little Mermaid
in Copenhagen, another city by the sea,
and of wanting her mermaids not to be as lonely.

More enigmatic was the sculpture
we created together of a young girl
on the cusp of adolescence
with slim flanks and bare breasts.
She has assumed the posture of Venus de Milo.
Her pelvis is tilted, and her weight rests
on her straight right leg,
while her left knee is bent.

We called her "The Hair Skirt,"
because she is wearing a pleated miniskirt
I made of photo-sensitized linen
printed with multiple images
of my "Phoenix Recumbent,"
a reclining female nude
with flowing blond hair.
Using surgical gauze and plaster,
Ruth made a life-cast of ten-year-old Addie
and painted her gray.
She is not only missing arms,
but a head as well.

Without any arms, Venus de Milo
is helpless to prevent the loose cloth
she wears from slipping past her hips.
In a moment it will fall,
and her full nakedness will be revealed.

Not so our girl. Her miniskirt
is secured by an elastic waistband.
Her hem skims the bottom of her butt.
She is both sexy and demure,
seductive and forceful.
Our sculpture created a minor sensation
when it was exhibited
in "U.S.A. in Your Heart."
Mine was the only photograph
not mounted on a wall—
two women, one older and the other old,
channeling youth, having a bit of fun.

BURNT STATUES

I   The *Moai*

It's a miracle they are here at all,
on a solitary island surrounded by ocean,
thousands of miles from anywhere,
with a volcanic crater at its center.

Monumental sculptures of long faces
carved from volcanic tuff,
standing eight to forty feet high,
the *moai* reach deep into the ground,
hiding and revealing secrets
of the people who made them.

Rapa Nui—a seafaring people
who came from Polynesia
a thousand years ago.
How did they find this speck
of an island in the vast sea?
Were they blown off course?
Was their journey intentional?
Their coming is a mystery.

By the nineteenth century,
the population was decimated,
killed by European diseases
or forced into slavery.

Today, the descendants live
in a vortex of climate change—
storms and surges, coastal erosion.
Trash from four continents
washes up on their shores.

On a ranch last year,
a fire broke out. Some know
who set it, but they aren't telling.
Wind spread the flames
to the sacred crater.
A hundred *moai* were scorched.

The *moai* are not eternal.
They can be rebuilt. A century ago,
their significance was forgotten.
Reclaiming their collective memory,
an oppressed people became free.
They recognized the *moai*
as representations of their ancestors
who walked the same land
they walk now, breathed the air,
and watched the ocean.

II   Rapanui pianist, Mahani Teave

As a child, I never felt isolated.
I thought my island
was the whole planet.
My introduction to piano
came from a visiting teacher.

People would arrive for a year
and teach music, theater, dance.
Then they'd leave.
To advance my artistic dream,
I, too, left the island.

In Santiago, Cleveland, and Berlin,
I learned from great artists.
I might have had a concert career,
but I didn't wish to perform
every other day in a different place.
Guided by my teachers,
my goal was always to find
the maximum beauty in music.

Ten years ago, I returned to Rapa Nui
to create a music school on the island.
I felt no one else would be able
to create this school.
I was the one who had studied
with the world's best musicians.
This was something I had to do.

Everyone here loves being here,
and those who leave long to return.
Nothing is truer to being human
than art and music.
Here on the island,
there is artistic blood in everyone.

BLUE

BLUE

Dusty, worn blue,
sun-faded house.
The ghost of the sea
breathes over it at night,
leaving a taste of salt.

When I hung up the clothes
I had brought with me,
I saw they all
were shades of blue.

This is the color
I come back to,
the very hue
of my soul.

HAIKU

In sunlight we see
the dirt that has been hiding
in the shadows.

WHITE LILIES

The heavy fragrance
of the white Casablanca Lily
mingling with the white Baferrari Lily
blooming in the ninety-degree heat
of my July garden takes me back
to an Upper West Side street corner
in the early morning winter dark
twenty-five years ago.

Once a week, before work on Fridays,
I hurried a mile downtown
to buy a bouquet of white lilies
from an old man who sold them
from the back of his white van.

He was a round little man
with a gap between his front teeth,
and a gold filling. He taught me
how to clip the sacs of pollen
on the anthers of the stamens
to prevent shedding.

He was one of those oddballs
who eked out a living
on the city streets in those days,
like the knife grinder
or the seltzer deliveryman.

After about a year,
I stopped going to buy them.
I never saw him again.
but he inspired me to grow
my own white lilies.

My mother hated lilies.
She wouldn't let them into her house
because they reminded her
of funerals and death.
I am not my mother.

In the summer of my convalescence,
I sit under the wisteria arbor.
The heavy flowers droop on their stems,
the air buzzes with insects.

After weeks of illness, of waking up
in the morning feeling sore and bruised,
I rose from a dream,
in which a beautiful young man
told a table of enthralled listeners
how he'd survived a motorcycle accident.

When I woke, I remembered the dream.
I felt rejuvenated, no longer in pain,
all the parts of my body
relaxed and released, like a pond
turning over in springtime,
or a lily perfuming the air.

BRIDGE OVER THE NOSTERKILL

I

The rippling waters of the stream
are like a thought turning over and over,
slipping out of grasp.

The sun is winking behind the white pine
as I lie on the bridge,
feeling its arch under my back,

watching the pattern of green leaves
against blue sky, a faint scrim of cloud,
and one soaring red-tailed hawk.

II

Out of the corner of my eye
I see you standing on the bridge,
singing the way you only
sing to yourself
when you are happy.

You don't like to be noticed
so I listen without seeming to.
May you go on singing
in my heart forever.

MEDITATION AT NORTH BEACH PARK, BURLINGTON

Thickly wooded Juniper Island
rises from the lake
within swimming distance from shore.
The sloping peaks of the Adirondacks,
misty blue and far off in the distance,
belong to heaven and not to earth.

From the beach I watch a storm
gather from the mountains,
then sweep over the lake.
Whitecaps form on the surface.
It is like the sea,
and it is not like the sea.

Rain falls in large drops
propelled by a breeze,
and a canopy on aluminum poles
topples on the beach,
somersaulting erratically.

Under a shelter,
students and faculty gather
at an impromptu party
celebrating recent graduates.
I eat strawberry-rhubarb pie
and think of the mountains, eons old.
When they were formed,
fault lines pushed yellow dolostone
above the dark shale,
the older stone above the younger.

Now I am older,
I want to impart history.
Shivering children in wet bathing suits
wrap themselves in towels.
Sometimes the young listen politely
and sometimes impatiently,
propelled towards lives
that haven't happened yet.

I feel my hold on life growing tenuous,
like those islands farther off—
the Four Brothers—like steppingstones
appearing to float in the blue
without moving at all.

STEADY

There are ways of being steady—
unmoving, like a rock,
or in an even motion,
like metronome or clock.

Practicing balance, like a tree
rooted and branching.
With intention, I found my place
and held it, trembling.

Another form of steadiness
is simply not to fall.
Be ready to flee or stay.
Change happens to us all.

HERE AND THERE

How do you get
to the edge of here?

Stay with your idea.
It will change everything.

Where do ideas comes from?
Elsewhere.

There is always an elsewhere.
Here is not all there is.

OFF THE GRID

Will death come like blackness
came to my computer screen?
It went dark and wouldn't turn back on.
Like CPR on a heart patient,
I tried codes to restart it.
Briefly it came on, sputtered,
then went black again.
In the morning, it wouldn't wake up.

When I die, I would like to disappear
into the surrounding silence,
but there is the problem of the body.
It doesn't disappear. It fails.

I am my body, but am I inextricable
from my body? I imagine my release,
invisible in the intersecting circles
of two hawks overhead.

I feel soft breezes,
and all that blows through me
is tinged with that mystery.

THOUGHTS OF ENDINGS

I — August 19

The sea beckons this morning,
blue and rippling, but the beach,
when I arrive, is not inviting.
Sand washed away in a storm
left gullies lined with rocks
collecting mats of seaweed.

At shoreline, a shape
sways back and forth
in the tide, the color of a rock
but not a rock, large, heavy, soft,
swollen beyond recognition.

Farther down the shore,
I wade through seaweed over rocks,
until I can swim out in cold water.
Gulls circle overhead. Cormorants
dry their wings on a rock in the sea.

My summer swims are numbered,
but I don't count them. The ponds,
lake, bay, and ocean I swam in this summer,
the pool at the top of a waterfall—
all welcomed me. All but this cove,
this morning. As I left the beach,
I passed a herring gull splayed in the sand,
its neck twisted at an odd angle.

II — August 20

I saw a young stag at the edge
of the lawn, browsing the bushes.
Its antlers wore a velvety sheen
in the early morning sunlight.
We looked at each other
for what seemed a long while,
his liquid brown eyes,
my blue eyes.

We stood perfectly still
until he meandered into a dark seam
between bushes,
waving his fluffy white tail.

Summer is playing with fall,
a cool breath of air, a square of hot sun.
The color of the sea is ultramarine.
These are the most beautiful days of the year.
As I watch them pass, I hold them close.

LATE SUMMER, BLOCK ISLAND

The air gray, still, and parched.
The rain, when it comes, is a sprinkle
dripping silently on the ground.
The mourning dove's call is backdrop

to the sea's suck and ripple
that speaks of longing
and sadness, buried hopes
like lost wrecks off rocky shores.

From the marshes comes the trilling
of red-winged blackbirds, in the thicket
the cardinal's chirp, the meadow lark's whistle,
chatter of a hawk chased by crows.

In the afternoon, sunlight behind
banked clouds glints off a sea
as pale as isinglass, reflecting back
my memories as I write,

until the day when words will be
all that are left of me,
words and images
and other people's memories.

Bury my body deep in the earth,
but may my soul roam free
in the shadows under the trees,
in the dancing hearts of flowers,

the setting sun and the rising moon,
the barred clouds and winds that move them,
the waters where I love to swim,
beloved haunts of my essential solitude.

ABOUT THE AUTHOR

Steady is ANNE WHITEHOUSE's fourth poetry collection published by Dos Madres Press, following *The Refrain* (2012), *Meteor Shower* (2016), and *Outside from the Inside* (2020).

Her other poetry collections are *Blessings and Curses* (Poetic Matrix Press, 2009) and *The Surveyor's Hand* (Compton Press, 1981); three chapbooks from Ethel Zine and Micro Press: *Frida* (2023), *Escaping Lee Miller* (2021) and *Surrealist Muse* (2020), and two from Finishing Line Press: *One Sunday Morning* (2011) and *Bear in Mind* (2010). She is the author of a novel, *Fall Love,* available in Spanish translation as *Amigos y amantes,* as well as short stories, essays, feature articles, and reviews. Born and raised in Birmingham, Alabama, she divides her time between New York City and Columbia County, New York.

www.annewhitehouse.com

Other books by Anne Whitehouse
published by Dos Madres Press

The Refrain (2012)
Meteor Shower (2016)
Outside from the Inside (2020)

She is also included in:
Realms of the Mothers:
The First Decade of Dos Madres Press - 2016

For the full Dos Madres Press catalog:
www.dosmadres.com

www.ingramcontent.com/pod-product-compliance
Lightning Source LLC
Chambersburg PA
CBHW021627120626
46545CB00002B/440